Heal Me

ABOUT THE AUTHOR

Brian Hunter is an American author and Life Coach based in Los Angeles, California. Brian is the author of *The Hunter Equation*, *Rising To Greatness*, and *The Walk-In*. Brian was acknowledged as being intuitive at a young age, and then later in life was recognized as having psychic ability. Brian has been a member of *Best American Psychics* and was listed as one of the top 50 psychics in the world. Brian has worked with people from all over the world, including celebrities and captains of industry. Brian was an original cast member of the TV series pilot "*Missing Peace*," in which psychics worked with detectives to solve cold cases. He has also worked as an actor and model in Hollywood and featured in various movie and TV productions. Brian's current focus is on his writing and life coaching, working with clients from all walks of life.

www.brianhunterauthor.com

Heal Me

Overcoming What Hurts Us Most

By
Brian Hunter

Published by

Rainbow Wisdom

Ireland

Copyright © 2020 Brian Hunter

All rights reserved.

No part of this publication may be reproduced, stored in a retrieval system, or transmitted, in any form or by any means, electronic, mechanical, photocopying, recording or otherwise without the prior permission of *Rainbow Wisdom*. This book is sold subject to the condition that it shall not, by way of trade or otherwise, be lent, re-sold, hired out, or otherwise circulated without the publisher's prior consent in any form of binding or cover other than that in which it is published and without a similar condition including this condition being imposed on the subsequent purchaser.

With thanks to Gerd for exclusive cover image
geralt/Gerd Altmann/pixabay.com

ISBN-13: 9781797942018

DEDICATION

Dedicated to my mother, who has lived her life with grace while always healing from something and helping others to heal whenever she could.

Also dedicated to everyone suffering in pain who need peace and healing.

CONTENTS

1	Heal Me...	11
2	Death of A Loved One............................	15
3	Suicide..	22
4	Battling Depression	32
5	Failure...	39
6	Battling Addiction	44
7	Life Mistakes...	51
8	Loneliness...	58
9	Loss of A Pet...	63
10	Facing Illness..	69
11	Loss of Pregnancy.................................	74
12	Broken Relationships.............................	79
13	Toxic People...	85
14	Sexual Assault......................................	98
15	Abuse..	104
16	Self-Esteem..	110
17	Estrangement..	117
18	Toxic World..	123
19	Anger..	126

CONTENTS

20	Worry, Anxiety, Panic	130
21	The Hunter Equation	135
22	Structured Task-Driven Lifestyle	144
23	Fear	152
24	Love & Empathy	159
	Also, By Brian Hunter	167
	Acknowledgments	170

LOTUS

The Lotus flower symbolizes
rising from a dark place into
beauty and rebirth
as this is exactly how
a lotus flower grows

Lotus flowers grow directly
out of muddy and murky waters
and produce beautiful
white and pink blossoms

PREFACE

While the thoughts, ideas, and advice in this book are meant to help you, they are not meant as a replacement for professional medical and mental health care. If you are experiencing serious mental illness, or feel like you might harm yourself or others, please seek professional help from your doctor or other mental health professionals. ***Heal Me*** does represent itself as a cure for any ailment, nor does ***Heal Me*** promise to provide any cures, or promise to 'heal' any ailments, diseases, or conditions.

National Suicide Prevention Lifeline

1-800-273-8255

CHAPTER ONE
Heal Me

See me, Feel me, Touch me, Heal me - The Who

All of us are in pain from something. For some of us it is obvious, and we live with it on our sleeve for all to see. For others of us, it is hidden deep inside, perhaps from events long ago that few or anyone know about.

There are various traumas we each experience in our own unique ways, but they all send us to the same destination of pain. We will discuss many sources of pain in this book, but most important will be our focus on freeing you from the darkest places that leave you trapped and hurting.

Nearly as horrible as the pain itself is the fact you may not feel you are understood. You may not feel your pain and suffering is even seen. You may think that nobody can feel your suffering or even relate to it. This makes us feel lonely and even more separated from the world.

Sometimes, even if we cannot make the pain go away, we at least want to be seen and understood. Compassion is the word, and yet compassion can be rare when it is most needed. Compassion is not feeling sorry for someone or showing pity. Compassion is a form of empathy shown to others who are suffering. It is not patronizing you with fake sympathy. Compassion is recognizing that your pain is unique to you and not something another person can fully understand. Yet, we still see your pain, and can feel it in our own way enough so that we wish to comfort you.

Giving comfort is not a fake act of patting you on the back and telling you it's going to be okay when we don't know if it's going to be okay. Comforting is the simple act of being with someone and showing support, even if you do not know if things are going to be okay at the moment.

This book is about seeing your pain and suffering. This book is about compassion and comfort. But this book is also about showing you specific coping mechanisms for dealing with your issues and suggesting solutions to free you from them.

I have seen a lot of suffering in my life. I have experienced some myself personally. However, I have seen much more through all the people I have listened to over the years. You are unique, and your suffering will be different from anyone else's. But maybe what I have seen, felt, and listened to from others, can help you.

Maybe you have placed yourself into a cocoon of isolation locked inside a cage. Perhaps it is time to transform into a butterfly. While it is your choice to transform or not, maybe I can help unlock and open the cage so that when you decide to turn into a butterfly, you can fly free and live life to the fullest.

It is time to heal your wounds. It is time to renew yourself, your soul, and your life. It is time to take your journey of transformation. Through empathy, I understand you. Through love, I want to heal you. But I cannot do it alone. You will need to open your own mind, heart, and soul to your deepest feelings, fears, and pains. You will have to love yourself enough to make the effort. I believe in you, and you should too. I know you can make the journey if you decide to.

Some of you have picked up this book because you are in pain and searching for healing. Others have picked up this book because they see someone in pain who is seeking healing. Yet others simply want to better understand pain, trauma, and the desperate need for healing the human soul.

I know some of you have been hurting for many years, while others of you have been hurting for a shorter time. There are some who watch the pain of loved ones and wonder what can be done. I admire your courage and desire to walk toward restoring peace in your heart and soul.

I know not everyone sees or understands your suffering. I know not everyone listens to you. But I really want to help heal you. Although I am not sitting with you in person, I am with you in spirit. I have provided my thoughts and ideas in this book hoping you will find them helpful. I have sat with you while I write this. I hear you now. I hope you will allow your heart and soul to listen. Use what serves you and leave the rest behind.

Yes, this book is about healing. But really, this book is about hope. I cannot walk your journey for you. I cannot cover all your wounds. But perhaps I can show you how to cover your own wounds, and how to heal yourself.

This book is not about you needing to depend on others. This book is about empowering you to depend on yourself. This book is about you believing in yourself so that you do not need to depend on others. You are not alone. I will do my best to guide you. But my wish is for you to gain the wisdom and strength to fly away on your own when you are ready.

I want you to be free. I want you to be free of pain. I want you to be free of control and manipulation from others. I want you to be free from fear. I want you to be free from all that holds you back. I want you free from struggle that binds you, so that you may embrace the struggle that enriches you.

Hope is an eternal light that will never be extinguished. Sometimes hope is a tiny point of light in a vast galaxy of darkness. The darkness and cold can surround us and make us feel that the hope is just too far away. But as long as you can see the light, you can move toward the light. I will endeavor to provide tools to help you move toward the light.

Some of you might think you can no longer see the light. Perhaps you think the point of light is simply too far away from your position in the darkness. I wish to tell you a secret. If ever you feel you can no longer see the light far in the distance, please know there is another light within your own soul.

The light within you is not seen outside but is felt within. It is sometimes covered with pain, doubt, and debris. But the light is always there. As long as you have a soul consisting of whatever divine source your belief indicates, you have the light within you.

So, if you cannot see the light outside, look for the light within. I believe in you and know it is there. Even if you no longer believe in yourself, believe in the faith others and I have in you, so that you can overcome, survive, succeed, and thrive.

This is a new day for you. Everything can start to change. It takes only one step forward, followed with all the other steps to come as we walk this journey. On this journey, you now carry hope as you engage in healing and search for peace.

CHAPTER TWO
Death of A Loved One

The death of someone we love leaves us devastated and hurting. It results in pain that scars us and changes us forever. This pain that feels like it will never go away can prevent us from living our lives. Examining this deepest loss is something we must do so that we can build a pathway forward. We are not moving on, but rather moving through. It is not easy, but we will make the journey. Let us do it together.

It was their time to leave us. They had to go. Why did they have to leave us? Why did they have to go? Why so soon? Please wait. Please come back.

We miss them so much. We needed them. We STILL NEED them. We are so lonely without them. Lost. Broken. How do we live without someone we need? Everything we look at and listen to reminds us of them. All of our senses detect the slightest memories of them. We are not sure how to continue without them. It is certainly not fair, and the pain is more than we want to carry.

Whether it is our life partner, son, daughter, mother, father, sister, brother, best friend, or any number of people, they were a part of us. Without them, we are broken and not whole. There is a constant pain that never goes away.

At first, we are not even able to function. Then we are able to function only in extreme pain and discomfort. After a while, we can function with a fake facade of normalcy. We might smile or laugh. We act normal and polite, but deep inside we still mourn. The pain is always there. It visits us at night before we sleep. It visits us during our lonely moments. It creeps up on us when we see or hear certain things. It never leaves, and it is always lurking.

Why does this pain never leave, while those we needed to stay did leave? Why are the ones we needed to stay, replaced with pain that will never leave? Why did God do this to us? Or the Universe. Or life. How could life be so cruel? What are we supposed to do now?

I know it hurts. There is nothing I can say that will make it go away. We cannot bring them back. Or maybe we can? Sort of? We can't live without them. So let's find ways to keep living WITH them.

Healing from the loss of a loved one does not mean forgetting about them so that we can move on with our lives. Healing does not mean fully accepting or embracing their death. Healing does not mean finding ways to stop feeling the pain.

Healing within our context here, means we find a way to keep them with us. Healing means we find ways to integrate their essence into our own soul. Healing means we still love them, and still feel them with us. Healing is about going forward WITH them, not without them. Yes, they are not here in physical form with us, but they ARE, and CAN BE, with us spiritually and emotionally. Our memories of them can also be with us and alive.

Their death reminds us that their life was beautiful. Their life IS beautiful. I say "is" because while their physical form is gone, their spiritual form is still alive and with us now. Life is beautiful and precious because it does not last forever. The most precious things are those that are fleeting. Those smells, tastes, and feelings that we experience for only moments, and then they are gone. We treasure them and remember them. Things that last forever are less precious and taken for granted because we know they will always be there.

Death reminds us that our loved ones will not be here forever. Eventually they, and even we, will leave. We are so blessed by the journey. We celebrate life for being so precious, and only by accepting and honoring death, can this be possible. So we accept death as part of life and part of the journey. We are grateful for the time we had with them in physical form. But it's not over yet. The journey continues. Their spiritual form is still alive and we can still keep them with us.

When you are ready, one of the first steps in our healing progression is to decide that you are willing and able to let go of them in the physical form. You must let go of the physical form in order to switch over and adopt the spiritual form. This is what we are going to do. THE BIG SWITCH. We let go of their physical form, and adopt their spiritual form. We integrate their spiritual form within us, so that we can always be with them, and carry them with us going forward. This allows us to move forward with our lives while still holding onto those we need to keep with us.

If you are still mourning a very recent death, it can be difficult to let go of the physical form and switch to holding the spiritual form. I am not going to tell you how long you should mourn their physical form. That is none of my business and nobody else's business either. People who try to impose "rules" for mourning and timetables do not truly understand painful losses. It is different for each person. However, when you feel you are ready, you should do "the switch" since it is a huge step in your healing process.

So, what about this "switch?" How does it work and how do we do it? Well, we first admit to ourselves that the physical is gone, but the spiritual is still here. We know who they were as a person. We know their traits and qualities we valued most. We know, understand, and feel their essence. Yes, we can still "feel" them. We know their smile, laugh, mannerisms, and very often what they would say in certain situations. So without realizing it, we are already in the process of the next step.

This step is doing an inventory and summary of their true essence. What did this person mean to us and why? What was it about them that we enjoyed most? What is it about them we valued most? What do we miss the most? We can keep those things and hold onto them. We can still have all of these things when we switch to holding onto their spiritual form. We decide what we want to gather up and hold onto from them.

We also want to honor them and their memory. Ask yourself what they would have wanted and how they would have wanted to be remembered. They must never be forgotten, and we will never forget them. Part of accomplishing that is by identifying what their mark on the world was, or what they wanted it to be. It might be as simple as how they treated others, or perhaps it is a specific cause or interest. But whatever it is, they will leave their mark on the world, not just in our hearts, but also in their concrete beliefs of things or ideals they worked for in life.

Now you are going to gather all of that up and see if you can carry it with you always, by implementing those items into your own life. You will take the essence of who they were and what they were all about, and you will make it a part of yourself. In a sense, you will carry their spirit with you by making a part of them a part of you. The spirit of who they were, and still are, will become a part of you.

This might mean some minor changes in your life such as how you deal with others, or what social causes you support. This can mean it actually changes your personality and interests to some degree. How little or how much you engage with it is totally up to you. But that is not all.

In addition to absorbing part of their essence, spirit, and traits into yourself, you will also learn to feel closer to their actual "spirit being." I am not going to get into a religious discussion about this, and I am not telling anyone what to believe in. However, I am leaving here for your consideration the belief that you can still feel close to their eternal spirit, wherever the person goes when they leave this Earth.

You may have decided to carry with you in life part of their essence of who they were and what they stood for. This in itself can act as a tool for connecting with their spirit. Feel the person as if they were with you. Open your mind. Maybe you can even sense what they might tell you now. Perhaps you can ask them a question and receive some sort of answer, or get a sign back in return. Engage with them. It might feel awkward at first, but practice makes perfect. Eventually you might feel closer to them and feel that you actually can sense, feel, or hear in your head or heart, them speaking to you or showing you signs they are there with you. Use this presence you sense as a source of comfort. You are not alone, and the person is not totally gone.

Once you have absorbed some of their essence into yourself, and you have built a spiritual connection with their soul, you have effectively switched to their spiritual being. Now you can feel them with you in some way. You can know that you have picked up part of them, and are carrying them with you into the future, wherever you may go. They live on through you. They are not totally gone at all. In fact, they might start to feel quite present.

All of this may not seem as easy as it sounds. It takes effort, mental consideration, spiritual belief, and practice. Have patience and love for yourself as you make this switch, and make your connections with them. It is well worth the effort. Knowing you are carrying their torch forward with you is an incredible honor and gives a sense of comfort.

Once you feel you have switched over to feeling close and present with their spiritual being, the next step is to gently move forward with your life. You are not leaving them behind because you now have them with you. Therefore, do not feel guilty about moving on. You are moving on with them, and they are a part of you now. They will get to be included within your new or resumed grand adventure in life. They get to live through you now. So do not be afraid to move forward. In fact, be excited to move on, knowing your loved one would not want to be stuck in neutral with you mourning and not living. They would want more adventures, and for life to move forward. They are with you in spirit hoping you move onward so that they can also experience it with you.

You can honor them by making the most of your own life, and carrying them with you onto new adventures. They are not being left behind, and you are not leaving them behind. You are lucky now, because you have them with you to provide comfort and advice into the future. You may not have had this kind of connection before they passed. So since they passed, you actually have gained comfort and strength through their spiritual essence remaining with you more fully. Take full advantage of it and call upon them whenever you feel scared, unsure, or need comfort. Look for signs and listen to your heart.

I know everything I am suggesting might not be natural or easy for humans to do. But the loss of someone we love is so painful and affects us in profound ways. It is necessary to develop new skills and abilities as a human so that you can evolve to the next level in connecting with the spiritual world, as your religion or beliefs allow. What I am suggesting can be done within any belief, so long as you respect the tenets of your religious and spiritual beliefs and rules. I am suggesting that doing all of this will actually make your faith stronger. It will increase your spirituality. It will increase your inner strength as a person. It honors your loved one. It helps you to move forward as we all eventually must do.

I know those of you who have lost someone are in deep pain about it. I know I cannot fix it with words. I know it will take time, effort, and practice. But I hope I have convinced you and shown you that there IS a clear way forward. You CAN become more accepting and comforted with these very sad circumstances. You CAN be proactive and gain a close connection with your loved one while honoring their memory. You CAN keep them with you. You CAN move forward in life and live again. That is what they would want you to do. That is what they NEED you to do. You have my sincere love and support in overcoming your loss. You will become a different and greater person because of it, while your loved one gets to live on through you. Death is only a process of switching between the physical form to the spiritual form. Life is actually eternal.

CHAPTER THREE
Suicide

Suicide. People do not want to talk about suicide. However, most people at some point in their lives have thought about it, or will think about it. Many people have had their lives touched by suicide. Therefore, almost everyone is in pain from suicide in some way to some degree, whether it be a fleeting issue or a life altering event.

The two largest groups of people for us to consider are those who have lost someone to suicide, and those who think about committing suicide. Obviously there are others touched by it as well, such as those who have had loved ones attempt suicide, those who have actually witnessed a suicide, or those who have deep feelings or trauma from suicide in other ways.

Many of you have lost a loved one due to suicide. We talked about losing a loved one in the previous chapter. Losing a loved one to suicide deserves a separate chapter because it is a very different and unique way to experience a loss. Someone actually took it upon themselves to end their own life. What must have they been thinking? Or were they thinking at all? What kind of pain must they have been in to reach that point? Why didn't they consider the people they were leaving behind?

I have written this book for you. But in examining our pain of losing others from suicide, we have to consider THEIR pain and thinking, in order to process OUR own pain. This tactic is correct, necessary, and relevant, because we can at the same time examine our own potential thoughts and urges toward suicide.

Yes, those left behind by a loved one who takes their own life, are left broken and sad beyond belief. But in addition to that, we are commonly left angry because the person had a choice to stay or leave, and they left us anyway. Does that mean they did not love us enough to stay? Does that mean they were selfish and inconsiderate toward us? We are left hurting in pain and we did nothing wrong. Or did we? We are also left with guilt of what we feel we should have done, or could have done, if anything. Devastation, sadness, anger, and guilt. Some people even feel shame. Some religions view suicide as shameful and even speculate that the person who dies of suicide might not make it into heaven. As if the loss could not be any worse, this indeed makes it worse.

The loss is not something that can be easily comprehended. Having a family member die of suicide is a club you do not want to be in. The pain of just the loss itself is overwhelming. But the fact suicide was involved reaches down into the inner depths of your soul, and rips out a piece of you that you thought never existed. You will never be the same again, nor will you ever think of death and suicide in the same way again. You will also be left with all the unanswered questions of "why" and "what if." Add to that the anger of "How could you do this to me?"

But here is where this discussion is going to take a sharp turn. Even knowing your pain, wanting to comfort you for your loss, wanting to say anything and everything to make you feel better, I cannot, and I won't. At least not in the way you would want or expect anyway. The reason why is because it is not about us. You are about to understand the real reason why suicide must be in a different chapter from the loss of a loved one.

The reason why is because suicide is not just about US losing and mourning. It is about them. It is about the one we lost to suicide. Only by examining suicide from their perspective can we truly come to terms with it, and learn more about our own potential thoughts of suicide. So although I hug you and share your tears of all our losses, we must now set our own loss and pain aside so we can examine the pain of our lost loved one.

Imagine the pain they must have been suffering. Imagine how their life deteriorated, or got to a point where they would consider suicide as a viable option. Those of you who have considered taking your own lives already know what this feels like. You know the answers already. The pain is unbearable.

Those of you who do not understand, might be thinking that it was the person's fault for their life deteriorating to such a point of despair. You might be thinking that there is always a choice regarding life decisions, especially of whether to take your own life or not. You might be thinking that if the person had reached out for help it never would have happened. Basically, you are putting the full burden and blame on the person who was in pain and felt suicide was their only option. Please don't do that.

Why and how can I even say that? Well, a person in the deepest pain cannot process information correctly. They do not see possible ways out. They may have looked and tried, but then did not see any way out. Or they may have been in so much pain that they could not even make the effort to look for a way out. Think of it this way. If someone is torturing you to try and get you to do something, you are likely strong enough to resist at first. But after a while when the pain increases, your strength decreases. Once you are on the verge of breaking, you can't even think anymore. All you know is that the pain needs to end. You will do anything to make it end. Logic is no longer a factor. THIS is the kind of process and pain a person experiences EMOTIONALLY when they are considering suicide.

It might be an impulsive pain or situation, or it might be a long-term pain that has built up over months or years. Many different circumstances can exist to result in different timelines and ways of making the decision to end it all. But the equation is simple. It is: Incredible pain plus hopelessness equals suicide. For those preferring a more mathematical optic it is:

Incredible pain + Hopelessness = Suicide

That is the equation. A person can very often deal with either incredible pain OR hopelessness for a period of time. But if both of those items combine in a perfect storm at the wrong time, then you have someone who is very likely at risk for suicide. Remember that equation. We will be using it.

So when thinking about our loved one who we lost to suicide, we must consider that equation. We must accept they had incredible pain that we may or may not have seen. We must accept that in their moment of decision, they saw no hope for themselves. Thus, they made their horrible conclusion and decision that cost us a lifetime of pain.

They were not thinking of us when they made that decision. They were not thinking of our feelings. Why? Because they were in too much pain to think of all the other factors surrounding them. Or in some cases, the person DOES think of how their actions will impact those around them, BUT they calculate that their incredible pain and hopelessness outweigh the impact to other people. Remember, it's not about us. It is about them. It is about the equation. This brings me to my next point.

Does this mean that suicide is a selfish act, as the cliché suggests? If it is only about them, doesn't that make it selfish? Well, that depends on how much of a narcissist you want to be. Here is why I say that. Think of a person being tortured. They are being drowned, stabbed, or their limbs broken one at a time. They are experiencing incredible pain. They see no hope of escape. They decide that all they want to do is die. Is that selfish of them? Or rather, is it selfish of us to label them as selfish? We do not and cannot understand the full nature of the pain they were experiencing. Therefore, we cannot accuse them, insult them, or judge them as being selfish. Perhaps most of us in their situation would have made the same choice. We don't know because we were not in their situation at that moment. What we do know, is that their equation had too much incredible pain and hopelessness. So they did it.

So no, I will not label their act as selfish. I won't be so arrogant as to judge them when I did not feel their pain or hopelessness. In fact, I will feel the opposite. I will have some compassion for the level of pain they must have been experiencing. I will realize that they may not have been thinking straight. Perhaps some level of mental illness could have been involved as well. If a person does such a thing under the control of mental illness, does that make them selfish? No. In fact, how about we all agree to not accuse our lost loved ones of selfishness or anything else for that matter, since we don't know the full circumstances of their situation, or how they felt at the moment. They deserve our love and compassion ONLY at this point.

And now I am going to make another turn in this discussion. Hopefully you have your seatbelt on. How about we also agree not to feel guilty for the decisions of others? Many of you might feel some guilt that you should have, or could have, done something to prevent their death. This is a natural response and thought. We would love to turn the clock back on such a horrible event and change history. But we cannot. So let's stay in reality and examine reality for what it is.

Here is the reality. The fact is that you are your own person. Your lost loved one was their own person. Each person has their own problems, issues, feelings, secrets, thoughts, decisions, and actions. You are not responsible for any of their thoughts or actions anymore than they would be responsible for yours. But yes, I understand you are thinking, "Yeah but maybe if I had said something," or "Maybe if I had not said something that I wish I had not said." "Maybe if I had done this, or done that, or not done this or that." Here is the problem with that thinking. First of all, it is easy to see mistakes in hindsight. Anyone can do that. But we do not live in hindsight. We live in the present, and all function accordingly. We ALL get busy and do not say or do things that we wish we would have. We ALL say and do things we wish we had not. We normally never even consider any of this. We are only forced to consider it in those rare instances that something goes wrong. You cannot think like that.

You have to accept that you were living your life as best you could under all your own circumstances at that moment. At the same time, your loved one was doing the same, and making all their own choices and actions. You are not responsible for their thoughts and actions. Read that line again.

They ended up making unfortunate choices based upon their own thoughts that were based upon the equation of pain and hopelessness. You do not control those things. So, it is not your fault. We all wish we had done more. We all wish we had reached out more, said more, done more. But that is not reality. Reality is that the loved one was in charge. In many instances, they might have rejected us, or pushed us away in some way. You cannot force yourself upon another person, even if it's a minor, if they don't want to listen. It will not work. Maybe we can't ever stop wishing we had done more. But we have to accept that we had no control over the other person, their choices, or their actions. They did it. We did not do it. It is not our fault. They did it due to their equation. Please let go of any guilt some of you might be carrying. Please.

Where does that leave us? To my count, that leaves us with a loved one who should not be blamed or labeled negatively for being in too much terrible pain and feeling totally hopeless, resulting in their decision. That also leaves us with those they left behind, who are not at fault in any way, because we do not control the other person. To me, that means we have two sets of good people. The first one was in too much pain before the event, and the second set is in too much pain afterward. Good people who felt and feel horrible pain. Both groups are deserving of compassion and love.

You deserve compassion and love for your horrible painful loss. Your loved one who died of suicide deserves compassion and love for what they suffered that drove them to suicide. Now you both have something in common. Pain deserving of compassion and Love.

So let's do that. And this is where we take another turn. Let us immerse your loved one and yourself in compassion and love. Do not be mad at them. Do not feel guilty. Let's decide to just love them. Love them for how we knew them in better times. Love them for the reasons we loved them in the first place. Love them for what they meant to us in our lives. Let's just decide to love them. Let us stop asking questions, feeling doubt, and being angry about the decision. All of that has just been keeping us in pain. If they were in such great pain and were feeling such hopelessness as the equation would suggest, then they deserve our compassion and love for that reason alone. Let's just give them compassion and love then.

Let us celebrate their life. Please be proud of the person they were in the better times. Please do not let any well-meaning ignorant person make you feel shame for how they died. Do not let any religious belief make you think they didn't go to heaven. Come on. If we are talking religion, then we know God loves all his children, especially those who suffer. I personally believe that all of those who die of suicide go straight into God's arms if for no other reason than because of the pain and suffering they endured. God comforts that. God always forgives and comforts. God would not forsake a soul that was suffering. If you believe otherwise, you better check your beliefs. We can agree to disagree, and all still get along as friends.

Your loved one deserves compassion, love, and celebration for their time here in our lives. Additionally, you deserve compassion and love for your suffering due to this loss. Please take comfort in the fact that your showing them love and compassion now, is felt by them now. Your love to them now can bond you to them now. Allow them to become part of you, as you can now lean on their spirit for strength and comfort in your times of need. Maybe they will have greater strength and wisdom now after their ordeal. Maybe if you listen to your heart, you will hear them giving advice or messages. I am sure they learned plenty. It is time to be proud, celebrate, love them, and take them into your heart for your own comfort. Please remember, it is not how someone dies that matters. What matters is how they loved, and how you loved them. Fortunately, that exchange of love is eternal and does not need to stop, even with them gone from Earth. You and they can find peace together through love.

Now let's take one final turn. I didn't forget about you. Yeah, you. All of you who have been reading and thinking, because you have considered suicide for yourself. You have been struggling in pain with little hope. You have had moments when you considered suicide as a possible solution. Now I am speaking to you.

I am not going to be cliché or patronize you. I won't tell you "Don't do it," or "It will get better." Well, okay I'm lying. I WILL tell you it gets better. It does eventually. Sorry, I didn't mean to patronize you or be cliché. Here is what I really want to do. I want to just give you the facts. Let's revisit the equation. Incredible pain + Hopelessness = Suicide. So this is not my opinion of how you should feel or what you should do. This is simply math.

So if you are feeling suicidal or have considered suicide as a possible solution, that must be because you have experienced incredible pain and hopelessness. That actually gives us something to work with. What this means is that if we reduce or eliminate your pain, you won't be suicidal. It means if you see there is hope, you won't be suicidal. Those are facts and that's math.

Therefore, that is what your focus needs to be. Your treatment, through either self-care or counseling, needs to be reducing your pain and seeing there is hope. Please think about this. Please reach out to someone who can help you do this. The concept is simple. Reduce pain and see hope. If you cannot do this yourself, please reach out to someone who can help you with this. Sometimes a friend or family member can help you with this without them even knowing why they are helping you. Or maybe you will tell them everything, and then they will help you more directly. Or maybe you can reach out to a counselor who can help you with this. But this is what your focus should be.

There is no point in ending your life by suicide when the solution is simple as reducing pain and seeing hope. By now you hopefully see and realize all the pain you would be putting others through by your actions. Yes, it's about your pain, not theirs. But you can reduce your pain if you work on the steps to do that. Then you can spare others of their pain also. There needs to be an examination of all the issues putting you in incredible pain. Someone outside your immediate situation might have some good solutions for mitigating some of that pain. Once you see that mitigating some of that pain is possible, you will see hope.

Here is something else to consider. A law of the universe is that nothing stays the same. Things are always changing. Sometimes they change fast, and sometimes they change slowly. But they always change. That is a guarantee. I guarantee that your situation will change. Guaranteed. So at this point, it becomes a function of time. But that's not all. There are often decisions you can make, and actions you can take, that can speed the time of change.

Anything can happen at any time, and often does. Things can happen that you cannot even imagine or expect. It could happen tomorrow. How do you know? You don't. But it can. That is proof there is hope. Please grab onto hope and do not let it go.

If I could only send my love and compassion to one place right now, it would be to you. You need it most. You deserve love and compassion like everyone else does. But right now, you need it most. I want you to make it. I want you to survive. I want you to stay. Why? I don't even know you. Here is why. Those who have suffered the most usually are capable of the most compassion. Our world needs more people with deeper compassion. So that's you. We need you. We need your understanding of suffering, pain, and the need for love, compassion, and second chances. I believe in third, fourth, fifth, and unlimited chances. You are entitled to as many chances as you are willing to stand up for. You should give yourself a chance. You deserve a chance at life again. You deserve to live without pain. All you need to do is work with the equation. If you cannot do it yourself, ask for help. Seek help. Get help. It's not clichéd or stupid. It is about you getting the help and tools needed to fix your equation. Reduce that pain and see the hope. Things will get better. Then any amazing thing can happen after that.

All of us are in pain in some way. We can change that. Let us allow love and compassion to do so. Please start now.

CHAPTER FOUR
Battling Depression

Some of you may be in a very dark place. Some of you may be surrounded by the darkness of depression. Maybe you cannot stop crying. Maybe you don't want to get out of bed or leave your house. Maybe you see no hope and no way out. Maybe you think your life is over. Maybe you want your life to be over. Nobody can quite understand all your pain, and there is no way to adequately explain it to others, nor do you have the energy to do so.

It is a heavy weight of darkness that feels like it will never go away. How can anyone have any hope if it will never go away, you might think. How can I ever get better if I have no energy to fight, you wonder. You just need the pain to stop. I understand, and I hear your cries through the darkness. I know you sometimes feel it's hopeless, but I come offering you hope. Your tears are an expression of your pain, but your human spirit is proof of the light that still awaits you in this life. It is time to get better. Come with me. I will show you the face of your enemy and we will conquer it together.

I describe depression as an insidious crippling monster that can leave you in constant pain. It is a heavy weight of darkness that covers you and cannot be simply washed away. The first step in facing depression is to realize that depression is nothing more than a monster that tells lies. Depression is a monster that lives inside your head, always lurking. It finds all of your deepest and darkest fears, insecurities, traumas, and vulnerabilities. It takes all of the information it gained from accessing these, and it whispers things in your head to trigger you into despair and paralysis. Depression knows exactly what to whisper in order to control your thoughts and keep you in darkness.

Depression wants to kill you. That is its ultimate goal. Depression hopes that if it whispers the right things at the right moments for a long enough period of time, that you will decide to take your life by your own hand, by substance abuse, or any other means. While it works to that end, its intermediate goal is to keep you in as much pain as possible, darkness, paralysis, and hopelessness.

Depression is an abuser. It wants to beat you down and weaken you enough so that it controls you. The control it seeks is to keep you from taking the necessary steps to leave it. Yes, just like an abuser, it does not want you to leave it. It wants to keep enough control over you so that you can't and won't leave. But unlike human abusers, depression rarely makes mistakes, and it never gets tired. For this reason, it is very hard to shake and to leave.

Usually when we examine why you are in pain, we look for what the core issue is that caused it. But in the case of depression, it really does not matter as much what caused it. It can be caused by many things, as you know. Everything in this book can cause depression, and most people at some point will experience some level of depression. So with depression, we are not going to focus on the core issue of what caused it as much as we would with other issues. Instead, we are simply going to focus on getting rid of it. The reason I take this approach is because although the core issues for causing the depression should be addressed, it is nearly impossible to fully address core issues while you are paralyzed and controlled by depression. So really, the depression needs to be brought under control first, before you can think clearly with the strength needed to fully resolve core issues.

The most important thing you should realize, fully accept, and remember, is that depression is a monster in your head that lies. This is critically important because you MUST become very cognizant from now on that everything it whispers in your head is a lie or twisted in some way. You have to stop taking it seriously, taking it to heart, and even listening, or paying it much attention. You have to call out its whispers as invalid. Like all abusers, depression relies on constant systematic brainwashing to keep you under its control. Thus, you have to break the cycle of abuse.

Let us say you are alone in your thoughts, and all of a sudden you feel that thick black cloud coming over you. You sense the monster is present. Then it whispers something in your head. It whispers one of its common thoughts it uses to trigger you into depression, anxiety, or panic. The first thing you need to do is think, "Not today, Satan." That is me being tongue and cheek during a dead serious somber discussion. But in all seriousness, you need to think, "Go away." "I dismiss you." "I am not listening to you today." You can come up with whatever thought works best for you. You have to realize it is just a monster using your innermost "issues" to whisper something that will trigger you into pain and paralysis. It is hoping to control you and eventually make you so despondent that perhaps it can kill you.

So right there we have called it out on its bullshit. We know what game it's playing. We know what it is, how it's playing, and what it hopes to accomplish. RESIST. DO NOT PLAY ALONG. DISMISS IT.

But beware. The monster is strong, clever, and does not give up easily. It will search and look for other inner issues and fears you have that it can try and use against you. It is trying to trigger you. So when you dismiss its first attack, you can expect it to make additional attacks in an effort to find something else that will successfully trigger you into despair and under its control. Therefore, be ready to receive these further attacks, and be ready to dismiss them as well.

The trick to all this, which takes practice, is to always expect it to attack and whisper something you do not want to hear. It will always try and come up with something new or a different angle on something old. But the one common underlying theme it will always use is HOPELESSNESS. Remember, it wants to kill you. Therefore, it will try to use the suicide equation against you by increasing pain and stripping you of hope. It will always strive to convince you that your life is hopeless. It will try to convince you that your problems and pain will never go away. You know this feeling, right? How do you respond? This is a test. REMEMBER, you must always remember that all of its whispers are LIES. So when it makes you feel that your life is hopeless, you KNOW FOR CERTAIN that thought is a lie. Everything it whispers to you is a lie. So by definition, you must not believe it when it whispers that your life is hopeless, or that things will never get better. In fact, if it specifically whispers that things will never get better, you should take that as great news. Why? Because everything it says is a lie, so if it says things will not get better, then that means the opposite must be the truth. It means things WILL get better.

Okay, so what do we have so far? Well, we know depression is a monster that lies, and just tries to whisper things in your head in an effort to convince you that everything is hopeless. We know what it says is a lie. We know to resist and dismiss it. But what about the constant sadness? Even when depression is "silent," it still leaves us in darkness.

The best treatment for darkness is light. I mean that literally. I find the best treatment and coping mechanism for depression is to go outside in the light. The next best thing is exercise. Going for a walk outside is probably the best treatment I can recommend. Obviously, you can go running, hiking, biking, or even just hang out in the park. But you should go out. It is no coincidence that depression feels worse for most people in the evening when it is dark out. So be out in the light as much as possible during the day.

This begs the question, what should you do when it is evening or dark? First, understand that the monster works best when there is a vacuum. There is actually some saying about how the Devil works best in an idle mind, right? A mind that is not occupied is the perfect time for the depression monster to come out and play. So the answer is simple. Do not leave your mind unoccupied during vulnerable times. Do not offer that vacuum for the monster to enter. When you know you might be vulnerable, make sure your mind is fully occupied as much as possible. For example, at night, you might want to have plans for such things as reading, watching TV, listening to music, playing games, or whatever floats your boat. Do NOT just sit around and be sad. If you leave open that vacuum of space, the monster will enter and will start to do what it does until it gets a satisfactory result of triggering you into despair and hopelessness. Do not even give it the chance.

Thus far, we have talked about how to cope with depression so that it no longer controls you. You might be asking, "How do I completely get rid of it?" This is more complicated in the sense that at this point it IS helpful to know what caused it. For example, if you are depressed because someone you love died, then the grieving process becomes a part of actually getting rid of depression. If you are depressed because you had a career setback, or you had a breakup, then you have to address the direct reason by making a plan to move forward from those losses by engaging in new adventures. Ultimately, a person has to let go of what is lost and reach forward into the future for something new. Obviously, you cannot replace or find new people to fix a death you are grieving. But in many cases, and really all cases, some sort of "moving forward" will become necessary.

However, there is another major element in getting completely rid of depression for good. It's called TIME. Getting rid of depression requires time. The more serious the depression, the more time it might take. While some people are depressed for hours, days, or weeks, others are depressed for years. Do not let anyone tell you that your depression has gone on for too long. How do they know how long your depression SHOULD last? Did they experience your loss or trauma? Are they walking in your shoes? Are they God? NO. They do not know and don't understand. So do not let anyone invalidate your depression, or intensity level of your depression. Yes, it can take years in some cases. But depression will go away. It always goes away or fades over time. Once you stop listening, the monster eventually gives up.

Many people ask whether or not they should take medication for depression. I am not a medical doctor. You should always follow the advice of your trusted medical doctor or mental health professional. But my personal opinion is that medication would certainly be warranted if you are thinking of taking your own life, or if you are unable to function in your daily life at work, school, or what have you. If medication is what keeps you alive long enough to get a handle on it, then by all means it's a blessing. Many people also need to be able to continue working so they have money to pay their bills, housing, and food. Medication can be the tape that keeps you together in order to keep your life together.

However, it needs to be noted that medication does not cure depression. Medication treats depression so that something even worse does not happen. Therefore, even if you are on medication, you should still follow the suggestions we are discussing, for coping with depression, and ultimately getting rid of depression. Medication is just a tool to help reach our final destination of being free of depression. There is no shame in using that or any other tools that work.

We discussed recognizing the depression monster for what it is. We discussed calling it out on its bullshit, and those coping mechanisms for dismissing it. We discussed treating darkness with light. Now we need to go back and spend more time discussing how to move forward in your life so that you can move away from depression and leave it.

It is very important you do not go backwards. Do not go back into the darkness of what caused your depression. Always go forwards, and always go toward the light. Always go in the direction of hope, and away from the darkness of the hopelessness of loss or sadness. Identify things that represent light to you. Perhaps it is an activity, a place, certain people, or hopes and dreams. The ideal element is a new adventure filled with what you see as light and hope. You MUST create something for you to look forward to with excitement and hope. Identify what that is for you. Go toward it. Even if you can only take baby steps each day, go ahead and take those steps. As long as you are moving, you will get there. Most importantly, you just want to be moving FORWARD. It is this movement away from the darkness and toward the light that frees you from depression.

I know you can overcome this. I know how much it hurts. I know it makes life seem hopeless. I know how it can go on for what seems like forever. But I promise you things get better. One thing you can depend on in the universe is that things always change. So if things are horrible for you right now, you can be guaranteed that will change. It is a law of the universe. Things change.

Also, the human spirit has an eternal light and strength that cannot be extinguished. The very fact you are reading this book is proof that through all the hopelessness, you do still feel deep down inside that things can maybe get better. I can assure things WILL get better. You can see that monster for the lie that it is. You can walk out of the darkness into the light. While the journey is not always easy or fast, the journey is always very rewarding. You will come out the other side a stronger, wiser, better person. You will become an example of what makes people great. Fighting through adversity and never giving up is what makes people great. You have the courage to walk through darkness, and the wisdom to walk toward the light. I believe in you, and you should believe in yourself. You will make it.

CHAPTER FIVE
Failure

Many people who are stricken with failure are so despondent over it; they cannot even find a way in their mind to continue on with life. Failure can create such massive depression that it can result in substance abuse, drinking problems, and mental paralysis. Very often suicide becomes a thought as well. Failure can make a person question their very existence. It certainly makes a person question their talent, intellect, and value as a person. Of the numerous topics, failure can be one of the most painful to many people.

Failure is a tricky subject. In my book *Rising To Greatness*, I talk about "embracing failure" as part of overcoming fear. In other words, we must fully accept failure to the point of embracing it, so that the fear of failure does not exist. The fear of failure prevents us from living our lives to the fullest and taking risks we should be taking in order to succeed and get the life we want. However, at the same time, failure is something that can cause us a lot of pain. Many people are tortured over failure for years, if not most of their life. We need to address that.

First, let's talk about what we mean by failure. For our purposes, failure will include things like getting fired, losing your business, bankruptcy, losing your home, losing all your money, and things like that. So we are not talking about losing that golf tournament you worked so hard practicing for and thought you would win. We are not talking about missing that new business account because your competition got it instead. We are talking real drop dead serious painful failures.

So the question would be, why does failure hurt so much? Why are we so affected by life failures that it can sometimes ruin us, cause us to give up, even trigger addiction problems, and cause us to go into depression and suffer for years? It is not because we wanted to win and did not get what we wanted. It is not because we are poor losers. It is not because we are spoiled brats and cannot handle setbacks. The real hard-core failures that cause us to go into deep pain are from something else. The failures that hurt most are the ones that were tied to our IDENTITY.

For example, if we based our entire identity of who we are as a person on our business or our career, and we lose that, then we lose our identity. We lose who we were as a person. We lose ourselves. Without ourselves, we are nothing. You see the problem? So this can happen with a number of other examples including that dream house that symbolized our life's work, or the money we had amassed through all our hard work and successes, or the respect we had in the community from holding a lofty position in government, business, or high society. If we lose something that we tied our identity to, then we psychologically feel we lost ourselves. We lost who we were as a person. So psychologically, we now think we are nothing. Pretty devastating when you think about it. So next time you see someone taking a major life failure particularly hard, you might have a better understanding of why they seem so destroyed by it all.

So what do we do about this? What happens if your career was your self-identity but that career is gone and you cannot get it back? Can you ever get your self-identity back again? Can you ever feel like a whole person again? Will you ever regain your dignity and respect within your own mind? How can you if you cannot get your old career back, or whatever it is you lost?

The answer is that you cannot solve the problem the way you have outlined it in your head. You have connected what you lost with your identity. You cannot solve your problem with that connection. With that in mind, the answer starts to become more obvious. You must detach that connection. You must detach and undo that connection you have between what you had and lost, and what your identity is (was).

That thing you lost is no longer your identity. You need to find a new identity. Yikes. Was that painful to read? Maybe. Or maybe not. Yes, it is much easier said than done. But on the flip side, it is a really simple good solution that works. If you can re-invent yourself and find something else to tie your identity to, then I promise you will start to feel better about yourself. What I should say, is that you MUST re-invent yourself and how you think of yourself.

A hard lesson to learn is that for most of us life is such a long journey that we will take MANY turns before we are done. Life almost never turns out the way we planned. Whatever you thought you had planned, you can almost guarantee it absolutely will not turn out that way. Life usually contains many phases, turns, and detours.

Yes, there are people we all know who stayed married to the same person, working with the same company, and living in the same house for their entire lives. Yep, it happens. But not to me. Probably not to you. It happens to almost nobody. Even if it does happen, something else usually happens we do not see coming, such as some family or health issue. Life is never as simple or clean as it can appear, even in the best of examples. More often than not, you will make many drastic changes in your life before it's all over.

Therefore, when you suffer a failure and lose something that you thought was the bedrock of your existence, you need to remember and realize it is likely one of those phases ending so that another phase can begin. It is likely one of those turns in the road of life. You have to pull back a bit and see the big picture of life. I'm sorry, but one of the laws of the universe is that nothing ever stays the same forever. The universe itself is always expanding, but we won't get into a cosmic debate right now. The point is that only a fool thinks they can keep everything forever. Everything eventually comes to an end in some fashion. Therefore, recognize that this is one of those moments.

It is now time to create something else. It is time to work for something else. Achieve something new. Attain new accomplishments. Try new things. Explore your ever-changing mind and passions. As we age and gain wisdom, what interests us often changes. Perhaps it's time to discover and explore new things you have had more recent interest in.

The bottom line is that it is time to create a new identity. No, I do not mean go into the Witness Protection Program and get a new driver's license and passport. I mean it's time to consider yourself something different than what you considered yourself before. You are not just a business. You are not a certain career. You are not a house. You are more than that. You are a human being capable of change, evolution, growth, spiritual awakenings, and higher learning. You are well equipped to change your self-identity to something new, and perhaps much better.

So you have to let it go. You have to let go of that old self-identity that is no longer relevant. Again, that is easier said than done. But if you don't, you will be one of those people who dwell in your failures for years. The easiest way to let go of your old identity is to adopt a new one. It is a great time to do some self-examination and ponder what you liked about yourself to this point, and also what you didn't like about yourself. You can evaluate your personal values and lifestyle of how you live your life, and what is important to you now, more than what used to be important to you.

Sometimes the businessperson goes into social work, and sometimes the social worker goes into business. The person who always worked with people might decide they now want to work with animals. The person who did sales calls might decide to work alone in an office, while the person always alone in the office might decide it would be more fun to interact more with people. You get the idea. Do not be afraid to make major changes. I know I gave a bunch of career examples, but the idea applies to all different kinds of life failures. A person who was always married, but got divorced, might now want to explore life as a free independent single person, rather than just find a new marriage partner immediately. A person who lost their home, might now realize there is a lot less work with renting, and more time to experience other things in life. Nothing is ideal. Nothing I am saying takes away from the pain of the failure or loss. However, we have to let it go and look in a forward direction now. The transition is not always easy, but the destination of eventually finding a new self-identity we are comfortable with, is well worth the work.

Again, what is failure? Well, our definition is now changed a bit from when we started. Failure now is a turn in the road. Failure is the end of an old phase so that we can start a new phase. Failure is our challenge, and our chance to create a new self-identity. Failure is not that bad actually. Failure is opportunity for change. Failure is nothing to be afraid of. Most of all, failure is nothing to remain in pain about for long. It is time to live and succeed again. Embrace failure as your precious opportunity to change your life into something even better and more meaningful than what it was in the past.

CHAPTER SIX
Battling Addiction

Addiction is something that some fall into as they are trying to escape pain, even though addiction only results in more pain. Almost every person is touched by addiction in some way, whether it be your own struggle, or someone you know is struggling or had struggled in the past. First, let me make it clear that this chapter is not a 12-step plan to free anyone from addiction. That would be an entire book, not a chapter. But we have to cover addiction because of its prevalence in our lives. Correction. We don't have to cover it. We WANT to cover it. And "wanting" to do it is the major requirement in addressing it. Many people need to, but do not. Those who want to, are the ones who succeed in freeing themselves.

We are also going to look at addiction from two different sides. There is the side of those who struggle with having an addiction. Then there is the side of those who suffer from being around those who struggle with having an addiction. Those from both sides are in pain.

Those who find themselves trapped in addiction did not wake up one day and decide they wanted to be trapped in addiction. They likely were escaping some other pain and just needed something to make them feel better, if only for a short time. Or maybe they were just trying to enjoy life as a party, have a good time, and ended up engaging in things others were doing around them. Or perhaps in a lapse of judgment, they tried something in a moment within an empty vacuum without understanding the full consequences. Whatever the reason, nobody wakes up and decides they want an addiction. To those escaping pain and making bad choices in doing so, it just kind of happens.

Yes, those of you who have never fallen into addiction are probably snarling and saying, "It doesn't just happen." "Poor choices cause people to fall into addiction." Well, actually both of those are true. Yes, it is a poor choice to engage in activities that cause addiction. But yes, it can just happen. Life circumstances can happen that plunge people into all kinds of trouble. If you do not understand this, it is only because it has not happened to you (yet), and hopefully never will. Life is always so simple and easy until it isn't. Then it is not. At that point, we can get into all sorts of trouble.

If you are stuck in addiction, I know you do not want to be there. Not all people understand how painful life can become. Sometimes you just cannot continue without some temporarily relief. But then this temporary reprieve is such an incredible euphoric comfort, that you just can't leave it. So you need to remain in that temporary state of relief for a longer period of time. If it feels good, you do not want it to end. It is very difficult in this world to feel good. Why would anyone not want to feel good? So you bathe in this relief, and it's almost a blessing at first. Except it is not. It is a liar and cheater. Why do I say that?

It is a liar and a cheater because at first it represents itself as something that will make you feel better, even if temporarily. But that's a lie. It will only do that for a short time. Once you have fallen into its grip, it starts to lose its "beneficial" effects. The pleasure ends sooner, and you need more, and more often, to gain the same pleasure as before. Then eventually, there is no pleasure at all. It becomes pleasure-pain, but not in a ticklish good sense. It gets to a point where you feel the pleasure of the substance/activity at the exact moment you feel the pain of the addiction. It has turned on you. Now it sucks. It is stealing everything from you. It may even be killing you. It no longer gives you anything. Yet, you keep doing it because you have to. The pain of stopping is greater than the pain of continuing, even though continuing means the pain will never end. Your ways out become limited, painful, and seemingly too difficult to face.

I know for some, I am being a bit overly dramatic. An addiction to meth is not the same as an addiction to gambling, porn, or food. All addictions are a bit different. But I think it's helpful to outline the true full potential struggle, and anyone with any addiction can still relate to what I am saying.

The end result is that you are now in more pain than you were before, except this time you are trapped and afraid that you can't escape. You now watch yourself destruct, either slowly or quickly. Whether you are taking hard drugs that could kill you any day now, or drinking alcohol that kills you over time, or you are smoking which will likely result in a horrible lung disease someday, you ARE self-destructing at an uncomfortable pace. Then, on top of all that, there are all those who have to watch you do this.

Let me now speak to those who are in great pain watching the ones they love struggle within this darkness pit of hell. You watch helplessly as you see the ones you love hurting themselves, self-destructing, and maybe even dying from what they are doing. You watch them lose their lives, jobs, homes, and families. You watch as they lose themselves. You wonder to yourself if there is anything you should be doing. Maybe you feel guilty because you think you "should be doing something," or "should have done something long ago." You wonder if there is something you can do now. How is it fair that the choices and actions of another person can cause YOU so much pain? The actions of another person can cause destruction in YOUR life, even though you are doing nothing wrong. It's not fair. It's painful.

Those of you stuck inside addiction need to realize that YOUR pain is not the only pain. There is also the pain others are experiencing watching your struggle, and even suffering some of the collateral consequences. People love you. You might think they hate you because they are not speaking to you, or they are not helping you, or they have pushed you away. Their frustrations and actions as a result of your addiction do not mean they don't love you. It means they cannot allow your addiction (toxicity) into their lives. They are already in pain from what you are doing, and they cannot bear to increase that pain by wading even deeper into it, especially since it is not theirs to own by their doing.

So let us all agree on something right now. Addiction puts everyone in pain. Everyone on both sides are in pain. Everyone wishes it would just stop. But the person inside the struggle of addiction cannot "just stop." Don't you think if they could just stop, they would? So obviously they can't. Stop telling them to just stop. They would if they could. They don't like it anymore than you do. They dislike it much more than you do actually. So let's not have a contest of who is hurting more, who is hurting who more, or who can stop it and who cannot. To a degree, everyone in this equation needs help to stop the pain.

Whatever your addiction is, minor or major, you first need to recognize you have a problem. Duh! That is the most clichéd statement of this book. Step one. Yeah, I'm a genius. Not! But it is indeed the first step. Really, the most important step of all comes next. You need to decide whether or not you WANT to stop or change. If you do not want to change your life, then you are not ready yet. But once you have had enough pain, gone in circles with it enough, and realize it's a dead end leading to nowhere, then I think you may realize you want to change.

This notion of deciding you WANT to change cannot be overstated enough. It is the most important decision you will likely ever make, because once you decide you want to change, you can change. You CAN change. Yes, you can. I say that because after being stuck in addiction for a while, the person starts to become convinced they can never escape or change. They often give up even considering it or trying. So the idea that you CAN change is a big idea.

Once you decide you want to change, you need to decide what level of help you need. Not everyone needs outside help, and it depends on the addiction. But many or most do need outside help to some degree. If you have a chemical dependency, you will need help in my opinion. This might range from a person watching over you as a babysitter, or it might involve getting a prescription medication from your doctor, or it might involve enrolling in a program which might be in-patient or outpatient.

If you have a severe chemical dependency, you will need some sort of detox that safely releases you from the chemical dependency. It does NOT stop the addiction or cure you. It simply gets the poison out of your system in a safe responsible way, and breaks the initial chemical dependency so that you hopefully will not immediately engage with it again right after getting it out of your system. Thus, if chemical dependency is an issue, go ahead and ask for help. Ask Family members, your doctor, or someone you know who has been through something similar. They can help point you in the correct direction to deal with the chemical aspect of this issue, including the detox.

Again, I'm sorry if I am being overly dramatic for some. You can use the concepts written above even if your addiction is minor or different. For example, a smoker will treat their chemical dependency by getting a "smoker's patch" or some other aide to help them. A person with an eating disorder might consult with their doctor or a nutritionist who can guide them into the beginnings of their journey to a healthier life.

Once you have freed yourself of the immediate detox dangers, and the immediate chemical dependency, the self-work begins. I say self-work, but very often it's best to continue getting help in the form of a professional program, or meetings, or counselor. I use the term self-work because it is important to stress that at this point, whether you succeed or not is up to you. It's about doing the work, having the correct structure in place, coping mechanisms, discipline, and most of all, lifestyle change.

As I said in the beginning, this chapter is not meant as a full 12-step program. Please do not think that I am discussing everything that needs to be discussed. I urge you to engage in a full program or counseling sessions to get weekly or daily in-depth guidance on successfully navigating yourself to freedom and good health.

With that said, my own feeling is that the next steps involve a combination of life structures, coping mechanisms, and examining emotional core issues. You should put into place a daily lifestyle that does not allow you to fall back into addiction. That might mean providing good separation between you, everything, and everybody that leads to your addiction. You want to place yourself in the right locations so you are safe from falling back in. You want to engage in activities that keep you busy, occupied, and away from falling back into addiction. You want to engage in activities that tend to be the opposite of addiction, such as exercise and nature. You want to have coping mechanisms set up so you have things you can immediately do, or people you can immediately call, if you feel in danger of falling down. You want safeguards in place. You want backup plans, and then backup plans for the backup plans. I could write a book just on this paragraph. It is very important and a key part of staying clear of your addiction.

Let me say this, and let me be very clear. Beating addiction is not just about seeing how long you can abstain from the addiction. The truth is that only depending on sheer discipline is not a very effective method. In my opinion, it is impossible to beat addiction unless you make major lifestyle changes. This might be the most important point of this entire chapter, so let me say it again a different way. You must change your lifestyle if you want to beat addiction. So, if you are struggling and keep falling down, it is likely because you have failed to make big enough lifestyle changes. Lifestyle changes include where you live, what you do, who you spend time with, and your daily schedule and routines.

Once the coping mechanisms and lifestyle changes are in place, you need to examine the core issues that caused your addiction in the first place. This is the part where you actually work to fix your issues instead of just treating them. Once you identify what actually caused the addiction in the first place, you can work to resolve those core issues, so that they no longer affect you the same way they affected you before.

Remember, there is always pain that causes addiction. Pain caused addiction, which caused the pain of addiction. So, you need to identify what exactly that pain or issue was that drove you to needing relief, which then resulted in the addiction. Lots of self-reflection and a very good counselor are in order. The job of the counselor is to guide and facilitate you on your journey to finding and examining those core issues. If your counselor cannot find a core issue if it sat on the tip of their nose, then find another counselor who can. Not all counselors are created equal, and some have talents for different things in different areas. Some just listen, and others try to push you to a certain destination that might not be YOUR destination. What you want is someone who will effectively guide you to YOUR destination through correct questions that lead you down the lighted path.

For those of you sitting back and watching all this because you do not have an addiction, but you are in pain because someone you know has an addiction, your job in all this is to show love, support, and encouragement. The person trying to recover from addiction likely thinks you are angry at them, hate them, don't understand them, or have abandoned them. By now, they realize they hurt you and that you have every right to not engage with them. You can be helpful by showing you enthusiastically support their efforts in recovery. The status or ultimate outcome of your relationship with them does not even matter really at this stage. What matters is that you love them enough to wish them success in recovering, and living a healthy life. Love them enough to wish them health and happiness, even if you no longer want them in your life the same as you did before. The recovering person already knows life has changed and life will be different. They expect some people will be gone and others will have changed. The focus really needs to be on creating the change, solidifying the change, and creating a healthy lifestyle on the other side.

To those who are struggling with addiction and reading this, the process

I have outlined is brief and leaves out some bumps in the road, but is still a very doable rough framework for you to follow. I hope you see that. It all starts with you deciding you WANT to change. Then follow the rough outline in this chapter, or seek help elsewhere that you feel will resonate with you. The underlying theme you need to remember is that you CAN change. You CAN free yourself from whatever is trapping you. You CAN start today if you choose to. I know you can do it when you decide you want to do it. Keep trying until you succeed. Relapse is often part of recovery. If you fall down, it is likely because your core issues flared up, your coping mechanisms failed, or your lifestyle changes and structure failed. Evaluate what failed and fix it so the exact same failure will not repeat itself. Then start again.

Sometimes the true success is found in the difficult journey. A person who tries and fails many times before they succeed, often has more solid results in the end because they suffered more, which means they are less likely to return, and more likely to have an in-depth understanding of the issues that caused their pain. So do not give up. Everyone can do this. You can do this. A whole new life is waiting for you. It is never too late to try again and start again.

CHAPTER SEVEN
Life Mistakes

Everyone makes mistakes. However, some mistakes are so big that they affect us for the rest of our lives. They leave us in regret, which leaves us in pain. Coming to terms with mistakes is necessary for releasing pain that serves no purpose to anyone.

I will not attempt to predict and list everyone's mistakes. I won't pretend to understand everything you have gone through and feel as a result of your mistakes. I will not ignore the fact that others may have suffered from your mistakes. But I also will not judge you or condemn you for your mistakes, as I hope you would not judge me for mine, or anyone else's. However, let's face it, people do judge us for our mistakes. They also condemn us. Therefore, we need to deal with that in this chapter as well.

Life mistakes are not about how you forgot to pick up the dry cleaning. They are not about backing your car into a light pole. They are not forgetting the ice cream at the grocery store, although that one can be pretty awful. Life mistakes are those rare life-altering moments when we spend the rest of our life wanting a do-over.

A life mistake might be that one time you cheated on your partner, which then ended your relationship. It might be when you charged something personal to your work expense account, and got fired. It might be when you were out of your mind, immature, stupid, and stole a car for a joy ride that resulted in you being branded a criminal. It might be when you had one too many drinks and drove home, only to get stopped and caught for DUI. It might be when you drove, or acted irresponsibly, and injured or killed another person.

Whatever your mistake was, you may have paid a heavy price. You may have lost your marriage, your kids, your home, your career, or even your freedom. Perhaps you ended up spending time in prison for your mistake. Perhaps someone was hurt or died due to your mistake. Perhaps you long since paid your price, or perhaps you continue to pay your price every day of your life.

Any way you slice it, you probably suffer deep down inside every day. If so, then you are still paying that price for your mistake. You might go to bed every night and wake up every morning wishing you could have a do-over. If you could just roll back the clock and have another chance, you would definitely do things differently and avoid that mistake. You promise yourself and others you will never make that mistake again, but it doesn't fix it. You feel regret as if it was flowing through your veins. You are sorry. But you cannot erase it. Even if you are lucky enough to fix it, you cannot erase it. You have the pain and regret of what you did, but also the pain of the judgment from others. You might deserve the judgment of others, but you wish they understood the pain and price you pay every day. Sometimes we are not allowed another chance. Sometimes people will always judge us and never forgive us.

This can eat a person alive. You might wonder why you are even alive if there is no chance for redemption. What's the point? Why don't they just kill you if they hate you so much, judge you, and won't forgive you? Is this your punishment? Is your punishment to live with no hope or redemption?

These are not easy questions or issues. There are no easy answers in many cases. But as with other issues we are examining in our lives, we have to base our examination of this issue in reality. The reality is that for whatever reason, we made a mistake. The reality is that we cannot change it. The reality is that we are still here. The reality is that we can live our present and future lives in a way that is productive and positive if we choose. We need to look at each of those items separately.

THE REALITY IS THAT FOR WHATEVER REASON, WE MADE A MISTAKE. We are human (most of us). Humans make mistakes. All humans make mistakes. Some of us make bigger mistakes than others. Sometimes circumstances put us in positions of being more likely to make mistakes. Sometimes we take lots of dumb actions that result in mistakes eventually. We can make excuses, or we can own our mistakes. But we must remember that all humans make mistakes. Accept it. You are human. You made a mistake. It does not make you unusual. It makes you normal. Even if your mistake was not normal, the fact you made a mistake is very normal.

THE REALITY IS THAT WE CANNOT CHANGE IT. We go to bed every night and wake up every morning wishing we could change it. We wish we had that do-over. We feel regret. We are tortured by it. But we cannot change it. We just can't. This step in our process of redemption is a difficult step. This step requires you to let go of the possibility of a do-over. You have to stop thinking constantly of how you wish you never made that mistake. In a way, you have to let go of the constant regret. It serves no productive purpose. Those wanting to punish you might wish for you to be tortured with regret every moment of your life. But the REALITY is that it serves nobody any purpose whatsoever. It does not fix the mistake and it does not help you toward redemption, nor toward doing good things in the future. You have to accept that you cannot change it. You have to leave it in the past. It happened in the past, and it belongs in the past. You MUST move your focus away from this and into the present and future, so we can move forward in a productive and positive way.

THE REALITY IS THAT WE ARE STILL HERE. Some of you might wish you were not still here. Some of you might have almost died, but somehow survived. Regardless of your exact situation, you are still here. You are on this Earth in this life. You cannot transport yourself mentally away to some other planet, as you may have wished or tried to do. There is also no point in contemplating IF you had died or IF you were no longer here. You are here. Deal with that as a reality you must accept.

THE REALITY IS THAT WE CAN LIVE OUR PRESENT AND FUTURE LIVES IN A WAY THAT IS PRODUCTIVE AND POSITIVE IF WE CHOOSE. This is the step that allows us to turn the corner and seek redemption. We must seek and want the notion that we can still take actions that are good and positive for ourselves, others, and the world. We can do things that contribute to the world. This last step is where most of your focus needs to be.

At this point, we have accepted that we are human and messed up big time. We accepted that we cannot turn back the clock. We accepted that we are still here whether we wanted to be or not. We now need to fully focus on what we can do at this point. We cannot change the past. But we CAN change the present and the future.

We do not need to be the person we were in the past, and we are NOT the person we were in the past. We are the person who we are today. Additionally, we can choose to be the person we want to be in the future. We are not in charge of the past. We have no power in the past. We are totally powerless and helpless where the past is concerned. However, we most certainly can decide about our present and future. Yes, we all have limitations. Some of us might still be paying for our mistake in some way that limits us. However, that is no excuse for what we do with our minds, our attitudes, and our intentions for the present and future. You can choose to be a good person and help others. You can empower yourself to empower others. You can make a positive impact. You can build a new moral platform from which you live your life. You can hold yourself to new standards. You can set new goals. You can work harder than the "old you" used to work. You have the power to change YOURSELF into whatever you choose. For someone who is so powerless to change the past, you CAN choose to seize all the power of your future.

Some will wonder about making up for any damage your past mistake caused others. While you cannot erase or fix the mistake, you CAN seek redemption in the form of taking positive actions, and paying it forward to create positive results. You can focus on creating productive and positive results in the areas where you felt your mistake caused damage. Even just mentoring others into not repeating your same mistakes is a way of doing this.

Will you ever "make up for" your mistake if you do all this? No. Why? Because you are not trying to make up for your past mistake. You cannot change the past. We had to leave your mistake in the past. So you won't make up for it. But what you CAN DO is create something very productive and positive in the future that helps OFFSET your mistake. You cannot go back and fix it. You can't erase it. But you can build something very amazing that helps even out the balance. You may never totally even out the balance, but you can contribute in a way that is substantial.

Let me give you an example. But before I do that, once again I am being very dramatic in my tone within this chapter. Some of you have made more minor mistakes that did not hurt anyone but yourselves. I realize that. Some of you have made regretful mistakes that are more like setbacks, rather than traumatic tragedies. I understand. I have written this chapter in this way so that it can address the more severe cases, but the more minor cases can still draw the same information and benefit. So forgive me if I seem overly dramatic and the tone does not fit YOUR specific situation.

Now back to my example. Let's say you made a mistake that killed someone. You can never make up for that. You cannot bring that person back, and nothing you do can make up for the loss of that person. But what you CAN DO is take actions that can work toward redemption by putting something positive on the other side of the scale. For example, you can mentor others at risk for making your same mistakes. What if your actions in working with others means that several other lives will be saved because the many people you mentored will not make those mistakes they would have made otherwise? On one hand, you took a life. On the other hand, you indirectly saved several other lives. There is still no equivalency because we are dealing with individual lives. Saving several lives does not mean it was okay to take the one life. However, it is a substantial action in a very productive, positive, and powerful way to help even the scale some.

That final example is what you hope to achieve. In other words, you are not trying to erase the original mistake. You can't. It will always be there. But if you make the right choices and focus, you can most certainly do things to contribute very positive results on the other side of the scale. That is called redemption. You have redeemed your positive value as a human. You have "made up for" your mistake in a substantial way, given your limitations. You did not fix your mistake. You may not have even been forgiven for your mistake. BUT, you took positive action that significantly contributed to a better world. You saved other lives. That's a big deal. We thank you for that. If it were not for you, those lives would have been taken. Are you a hero? Maybe not. But are you appreciated and valued? YES. Yes you are. You are not appreciated and valued for who you WERE, but you are appreciated and valued for who you are NOW.

You transformed into the new person you are now. You are not the old person who made the original mistake. You are a new person who lives life in a totally different way under a different set of values and rules. It takes time, but people can respect you as the new person you have become.

Again, I know not all of you have killed someone. But the principles remain the same even if you stole something, cheated, lied, made a horrible innocent mistake that had huge consequences, lapse in judgment, or what have you. You can compensate by taking positive actions and paying it forward to contribute something to others or the world. Put something positive on the other side of that scale. That's what this is all about. It's not about trying to take away the negative on the first part of the scale. You cannot do that. Your only chance is to focus on putting something positive on the opposite end of the scale.

The journey in transforming yourself and seeking redemption changes you. The results you eventually produce change the perception others have of you. I personally believe that people deserve second, third, fourth, and more chances. If your heart is in the right place and you seek to contribute something positive to the other side of the scale, you deserve the chance to do so. I respect those who endure their mistakes, but then step up and contribute something great and positive to the other side of the scale. Redemption.

CHAPTER EIGHT
Loneliness

For some people, one of their greatest fears is being alone. Notice how I said "fears," not pain. I actually think the fear of being alone is worse than the pain of being alone. But then again, there is a difference between being alone and being lonely, just as there is between being alone and being in pain. Certainly, not everyone who is alone is in pain.

The first thing we need to decide is if you are in the category of fearing loneliness, or if you are in pain from loneliness. The goal is to neither fear loneliness, nor be in pain from it, in addition to being comfortable when you are alone.

As you know, I have a habit of over generalizing everything. Of course, I do this in an effort to keep things simple and to the point so that I can explain things clearly in an effort to be helpful. Phew, what a mouthful. So this is me acknowledging that I am aware that some of my generalizations are too general. But to cover this topic in one chapter, that is what I am going to do.

In my view, there are pretty much two common circumstances of loneliness. The first is when you are not partnered up with a romantic partner. Either you have not found your soulmate yet, or you ended up alone after a broken relationship. The second common circumstance involves older folks who lost their partner and perhaps do not have any children nearby who check on them often.

PLEASE, all of you folks living happily single and alone, note that above I am referring to "loneliness." I am not referring to "living alone." There is a huge difference. People living happily alone by choice or circumstance, are not in pain from loneliness, therefore this chapter may not apply to them. So I am not inferring that everyone who is alone is lonely.

Let's talk about all of you who are feeling lonely because you are currently single and alone. Those who have come out of long-term relationships can feel especially hurt and traumatized from loneliness. You are not used to being alone. Your mind has been conditioned to never be alone. You have always had someone with you or nearby. This is a matter of mental conditioning.

You may have noticed that in many of these chapters, a recurring theme is mental conditioning and brainwashing. The human mind is very easily conditioned to certain circumstances. So if you are always in some sort of relationship, and never alone, then your mind will be conditioned to that. Your mind will not easily accept being alone.

When we talk about being alone or lonely, there are two issues. First, the fear of being alone, and then the actual coping skills involved with being alone. If you fear being alone, you need to ask yourself why. Are you lacking confidence in your ability to take care of yourself? Are you so boring or such bad company that you don't like being with yourself? Basically, harshly, and crudely, you either don't have confidence in yourself, or you don't like yourself. Or, maybe it just could be that you have been unable to adjust your mental conditioning to being alone.

We need to fix these things. The best way to conquer fears is to face them head on. The best way to have coping skills for something is to force yourself to develop them. Every human should be raised or trained to live life by themselves for periods of time, such that they can take care of themselves. This is why it's actually a good thing for everyone to experience being single and self-sufficient at some point in their life. Obviously, the earlier in life this is experienced the better.

I urge you to identify any specific fears of being alone you have, and face them. Whatever you fear most, that is what you should walk toward and engage with. Whether it be handling your own finances, doing all the shopping, errands, and chores on your own, or entertaining yourself on the couch each evening on your own; you should go ahead and tackle it, and get comfortable with it. If you can eliminate your fear of being alone, you can usually rid yourself of any pain from loneliness.

However, some people are not afraid, but they are in pain from loneliness just due to circumstances. They can function alone just fine and do not fear it, but it might make them sad and result in pain of loneliness. Older people who have lost their partners and have no family nearby might fall into this category. For these folks, it is important to develop coping mechanisms.

There are different coping mechanisms, and each person needs to do what works for them. One size does not fit all. However, I will share with you a couple of my favorites. First, is to maintain a very healthy daily/weekly structure. You should be keeping yourself busy with productive tasks, exercise, time outside, and some social activity where you can find it. You should not wake up each morning with no plan, feeling lonely, and bored. You should wake up each morning knowing you have an entire day planned with your regular activities. You want to stay very busy with a good balance between productive tasks and enjoyable moments. You can have your morning rituals and coffee or whatever, and then get ready for your day. Make yourself busy with tasks that need to be done. Make time for exercise. Make time for getting outside. Enjoy nice meals. You might cap-off the night with TV shows or a book you really enjoy. You want to make sure you have a very full day, as well as certain special activities or treats you do on certain days of the week. In a sense, you want to enjoy living with yourself, just as you would with a partner.

The other coping mechanism I like to employ is something I call "Me, Myself, and I." I am never alone because I am always with me, myself, and I. We all keep each other company. I enjoy myself. I like my own company. I muse and laugh to myself about things. I like to think about things, and consider and muse upon them intellectually. I talk to myself in my head (and sometimes out loud). Yes, maybe I am a little crazy, but you need to be a little crazy to survive this world. My point is that I am never alone. I have myself. I do things that I enjoy doing. I give myself treats I enjoy. I plan things I know I will enjoy doing, or things that will benefit me in some way. I engage in self-care. I have my own routines and traditions I engage in that I really enjoy. I play music, watch TV shows, and enjoy fresh air, the sun, and nature. I never feel totally alone even though I am totally alone. I never feel alone because I have myself, along with me and I. We are all buddies.

This method or type of thinking is not for everyone, but it often works well because it conditions you to be comfortable with yourself, and to like yourself. So if three of you are not enough, you can always add a fourth called "yourself." Yeah okay, I have been annoying enough about this method and you get my point.

It is very important that you like yourself. It is important you like being with yourself, and like your own company. If you don't, then why? You need to identify what it might be that you don't like about yourself. Why don't you want to be alone with yourself? What makes you feel uncomfortable or sad? You need to really dive into some self-psychology. You need to get to know yourself, your strengths, and your weaknesses. If there are things you don't like about yourself, work on changing them.

There is no need to fear being alone if you face it and explore the issue fully. There is no need to dislike being alone if you employ some coping mechanisms and structures that allow you to actually enjoy being with yourself by yourself.

Some of you might be thinking, "isn't it just easier to find someone to be with so that you are never alone?" That might allow you to skip this entire chapter, right? Well, yes. BUT, our goal is to solve your core issues of pain. If you simply jump back into another relationship just so you won't be lonely, that is unwise and does not solve your core issues involving being lonely. It is better to do things right and solve the problem. This way you are not depending on another person to make you feel okay. Once you start depending on other people for things, you fall under their control, and you become vulnerable to losing that crutch.

I actually want you to become self-sufficient, independent, and self-empowered. I do not want you to be vulnerable. I do not want you to keep repeating bad behaviors or relationships, just so you can avoid loneliness. I do not want you to depend on others and leave yourself open to control and manipulation. I do not want you to feel desperate or weak. I want you to face the difficult issues head on and conquer them so that you are a stronger person who does not need another person or relationship for a crutch. Enter a relationship because it is right, not because you fear being alone or cannot cope with being alone.

The point of healing yourself from loneliness is not to accept being lonely, or being alone. The point of healing yourself from loneliness is so that you become a stronger more empowered person, who likes themselves, and who does not depend on others to fill holes in their soul or lives. Nobody who is alone should feel lonely or suffer pain from it. You can become more comfortable with it, such that it actually makes you a better person. So it is not about dealing with a weak or sad position in life. It is about using your current circumstances as an opportunity to become a more amazing stronger person.

CHAPTER NINE
Loss of A Pet

Most of us at some point experience the loss of a pet. It can be very devastating. But a pet is a pet is a pet? NOOOO. Here is the truth. At first, I was not going to do a chapter on the loss of a pet. Not because I did not think it was worthy. Quite the opposite. In fact, my thinking was that this topic was already included within the chapter of losing a loved one. I have always considered pets loved ones and members of the family. But then I got to thinking about how the loss of a pet can be even MORE devastating than the loss of a person we know. I will say what some are thinking but are too afraid to say out loud. The reality is that many of us have mourned the loss of our pet more intensely than we have mourned some of our extended family members. We won't make it personal and name names. However, some of us might have grieved for a day or more over an extended family member whose time had come, but we grieved for weeks and months over a pet. You can say I am horrible if you want, but I bet many of you would back me up on that. Conversely to that, there are people out there who don't think grieving over a pet is appropriate or really a major issue. These are often the same folks who don't think our pets have souls, which go to Rainbow Heaven after they pass. Therefore, due to all of the above, our pets clearly deserve and need their own chapter.

We are all in this together. We have loved, lost, and mourned. Some of us have been through this cycle multiple times. Some of the losses are harder than others, but they all hurt. Furthermore, there is always that one or two that affected us so deeply, we were too devastated to function in daily life for a period of time. So let's start with that.

You are totally justified in mourning for your pet as you would a close family member. Do not let anyone tell you otherwise, or shame you into thinking you are weird or weak for grieving your pet. As with other loved ones, the length of grieving varies, and your own amount of time needed to process and deal with the loss, should be respected.

I personally respect people's loss of a pet the same way I would a family member. People deserve condolences and any extra gesture of kindness you want to offer. Please do not think it's silly or over-dramatic. The loss of a pet can cause us such grief that we cannot get to work or even get out of bed. That level of grief and pain deserves compassion and respect.

With all that said, I think it is helpful to look at the passing of a pet with some perspective so that we can process the loss in a healthy way. As with any loss, an extended time of grief can cause us problems with our job, family life, and our own enjoyment of life. It is important to grieve in a healthy way so we can be ready to live happy joyful lives again, while we keep the memory of our lost one in our hearts forever.

When it comes to pets, I think it is very important to keep in mind and accept the cycle of life right up front. When you sign up for taking a pet into your home, you have to realize that you are receiving a loved one with a limited life span. I really think it helps to process all of this up front as you are taking in your pet at the beginning.

I like to build a structure of perspective about all of this. If I get them after they are born, I know I will have this cute little creature, and enjoy watching them grow into adulthood. I will then hopefully have many good years to enjoy my pet during their time of adulthood. But eventually, my pet will become older and enter the final stage of life. They may be elderly and have health problems for some time. I will need to deal with those health issues. Then sadly, the day will come that their journey with us comes to an end. Nothing can make us feel okay about this. Nothing can take away the sadness. But we must accept it and know it is coming.

Then very often, we start the cycle all over again by welcoming a new member to our family. We end up loving the new member just as much, but perhaps in different ways. Each pet is unique and important to us in unique ways. It is not about loving one pet the same as the last one, nor loving one more than another. It is about loving each pet the way we do, however it may differ from one to the other. One thing for sure is that we will love the new one just like we loved the old one who passed on. I think this is an important point to remember.

When we suffer a loss and our pet passes on, we must remember that there can be a new one right around the corner that we can love just as much. Sometimes we do not think that is possible, or we do not want to think that way. We want our old one back again. We will never love any pet again like we did our last one we lost, right? Well, not exactly. Those of us who have been through a few cycles know that we do end up loving our new ones a great deal. We still love and miss our old ones, yes. But our grief is often smoothed over by the love of a new one. There I said it. Gasp. It's true though. I have found that one of the best ways to deal with the grief of losing a pet is to get another one we can love. In fact, I often recommend that people get a new one before the old one passes. This way some of the personality and habits of the old one might rub off to the new one. It allows the old one to pass the torch to the new one. It also means that when we lose our old friend, we are not left totally alone with a house void of any pets. In our horrible grief for our old friend, we can lean heavily on the comfort of the newer family member. It makes for a slightly less dramatic loss, and more comfort available to us through the newer one.

Whether you choose to get a new one before the old one passes, or wait until after the old one passes, I find bringing a new one in quickly helps a great deal. You are not being disloyal to your old pet. There is no one-year mourning period where you have to wear black and cry for a year. Your old pet knew nothing but love for you. Your old pet would want you to be loved. The easiest way to accomplish this is bringing in the new generation who can love you as the old generation did. The cycle continues.

Thus, it is all about recognizing and respecting the cycle of life. Know that we enjoy them as much as possible while we have them. Then when it's their time, you send them off with as much love as you can. You can continue the cycle of love with a new one if you so choose and your circumstances dictate.

I truly believe the pain we feel from the loss of a pet should be turned into love and gratitude toward our old pet. We can continue the cycle of love with a new one. We can repeat this cycle over and over, knowing the end result each time is loss. But we also come to realize the end result is an amazing feeling of gratitude for all the good years and love we received from our pet. The cycle of life dictates that the old fade into Heaven, and the newly born get their chance at the adventure we call life. We should enjoy the process and respect the cycle. By doing this, we honor the life and memories of all our pets that shall come and go during our own lifetimes.

Many years ago, I wrote a poem to express my feelings over the loss of a very beloved cat. I will include that here to honor all or our pets we have lost, and to honor the cycle of life that we must accept and respect.

TIME EXPIRED

Now in the beginning I was presented with a tiny newly born kitten
I was "told" I would have 15 years and then I would lose him
They asked me if I agree to that
I said yes I agree
15 years is a lifetime away, so who cares... I agree
The years went by. 15 years in fact
Then I knew the end was coming, but I still enjoyed him

I asked if I could have another year
They said no
I said, well what if I offer you this money, can you give me 6 more months?
They said, you can do what you want, but you can't buy more time
Then it came that I thought I only had a day or some hours left
I had him on my lap that night the entire time as my remaining time suddenly had become more valuable
I enjoyed him
Then I put him on my bed for us to sleep
I thought I had hours
Then I said, can I have more time please
And they said no
I said...but it was 15 years...what is another day?
Another day is nothing
Why can't I have it?
And the answer was...your time has expired
You used your time
I said, come on...it's been 15 years...can't you give me a few more hours?
No answer
Then I woke in the night with him dying
I said...please...can I have 5 more minutes...please
And they said no
Your time has expired
I said...come on it was 15 years, so what is another 5 minutes....
They said...your time is over
Then I knew he was dying or dead
And I said...
Please...can I have 3 more seconds
Just 3 seconds to feel his fur
I said...it was 15 YEARS
What is only 3 more seconds???
And they said...sorry...your time has expired

And he was dead
I mourned. My time had expired.
Because 15 years turned into only another 3 seconds
Because eventually everything expires
And when it expires it means there is no more
Not even 1 second
No more time at all. None. 0
I used all my time. I used the last second. Then I had none left. And he was gone.

CHAPTER TEN
Facing Illness

Aside from the physical discomfort and pain, illness causes emotional pain for both the afflicted and those loved ones watching. Thus, we need to look at this issue from both sides. For the purposes of this chapter, we cannot really delve into the physical pain and medical treatment end of things. That can be for another book. Instead, we will remain focused on the mental and emotional pain suffered by the person who is battling illness, and the loved ones who are involved with the process having to bear witness to it.

I cannot wave a magic wand and make all pain and discomfort go away. I cannot tell you in a sentence what treatment will make your illness go away. But after giving this issue some thought, I wanted to approach this in a couple different ways. First, I want to see if we can give some meaning to our suffering. Secondly, I want to pay tribute to those who suffer from their afflictions.

Some of you have mild manageable chronic illnesses. Others of you are battling significant chronic or acute serious illnesses. Yet others are challenged with possibly life-threatening or terminal illnesses. I realize the situation is different for each person. But what they all have in common is this sense of "why?" "why me?" or "will it ever end?" It is unfair that any person must suffer. Even if you would not consider yourself to be suffering, you likely feel very limited by your illness.

Illnesses, whether they be a bad knee, or more systemic auto-immune type diseases, all limit our activities. They limit our ability to fully live our lives the way we would like. In fact, I think most people would say they can put up with the discomfort and pain, but it's the limiting factors that hurt the most. If you cannot go places and do things due to your illness, that is really the worst part for most. Thus, there is this frustration of losing quality of life, while also having moments when you feel like crap, and are in actual pain.

So what is a person to do? Let's assume for a moment that you are pursuing all medical options available. You are doing the best you can in that respect. So what you are left with is making the best of a given situation. As far as I am concerned, I see this as a quality of life issue. Coping with an illness is all about taking actions and using coping mechanisms in order to maintain the highest quality of life possible under your circumstances.

This really means setting aside the "why" and "why me" thoughts, and instead focusing on how to keep your quality of life as high as possible. Yes, you have to remain in the confines of your limitations. But you can reinvent yourself, whether temporarily or permanently, and discover a new life routine that you enjoy. This is really how I see it. I do not see illness as a devastating blow from which you must feel defeated and mourn. That would just drag you down and make you feel even worse. I really see it as a matter of changing your lifestyle, life structure, routines, activities, and hobbies, so they are in alignment with your limitations, but also provide you with comfort and enjoyment.

You should take inventory of activities and routines you can still enjoy, even given your limitations. Write things down, make lists. Always look on the positive side, and how you can maybe do things that you always wanted to do, but were always too busy to do in the past. Now is the time to take on those other tasks. An example might be that you can no longer go hiking up mountains, but you can do that picture album project you always wanted to do, but never had the time. You need to think more like that. Or maybe now you can become more engaged in the lives of your family, extended family, and friends, whereas before you might have been too busy. Now you can check on everyone and really make a difference in their lives with your love, attention, and support for them. You are basically replacing the things you can't really do anymore with other new things that you always wanted to do or might want to try now. The new things might even be more enjoyable and meaningful than the old things you did. Not all of this has to be a bad thing. Much of it can be a good thing if you think about it enough and re-invent.

I also mentioned this notion of assigning some meaning to your struggle. What do I mean, "assign meaning?" It means to consider what your present circumstances are teaching you as a person, and how you can teach others as well. Through struggle and pain, we become much wiser and usually gain more empathy for others.

This struggle you are being put through is a way for you to learn more about yourself and about life. It might even make you a bit philosophical. Do not let it make you angry. It is all part of your journey in life on this planet. A human soul is here to gain all kinds of diverse experiences and gain wisdom. Facing challenges and struggles is all part of that. So consider what you are learning from the experience. Consider how your discomfort and situation might be increasing the understanding and empathy you have for others, and changes how you view life. Consider the fact that you likely now have more thoughts, wisdom, and advice to give unto others for their benefit.

I don't know about you, but I don't have much interest in talking to people who brag about how perfect their life is. I get very little out of that except maybe annoyed. But what I do enjoy, is talking with people who have faced many challenges, struggles, and pain, and they are still here to talk about it. I love to hear how their struggles changed them and how they were able to get through it. That is very interesting and valuable wisdom and experience. So become that person. Become the wise inspiration that people look up to when they are hit with struggles of their own.

Those of you who struggle with illness are an inspiration. How do you do it? We know it hurts. We know it sucks. Some people actually fear what you live with every day. I do not look upon you as weaker or broken. I look upon you as a hero for living with your pain and limitations. I wish you did not have to deal with your challenge, and I hope your condition improves or is cured. Obviously. But while you are coping with your challenge, I pay tribute to you for dealing with it in a positive courageous way.

We have all seen those with various illnesses and diseases struggle with discomfort and inconvenience every day. But they deal with it the best they can. They keep going. They very often prevail eventually. We admire your strength and patience to cope with all you deal with. We learn from you. By watching you, we see what being a stronger more determined person looks like. We see courage and strength in what you do. It makes us better people to witness how to handle challenges one is dealt. So as you struggle with your limitations and pain, know that you are setting an example for others on how they might deal with it someday if they are in the same situation as you. Please continue to be strong and exude your strength and kindness despite your circumstances. It is inspirational.

For those of us who must watch someone we love struggle in this way, it can be very difficult. We might not have an illness or deal with the pain and limitations, but it pains our heart to see someone we love being afflicted in this way.

The best way to handle this as the spectator is to not feel sorry or scared. The best thing to do is respond with love, support, comfort, and encouragement. Nobody wants to hear you say how sorry you are over and over again. It's actually kind of depressing. What people want to hear you say are constructive things that feed into the person's effort to sustain and improve. Keep it positive. Keep it relevant. Keep it productive.

Instead of an attitude that is like, "oh you poor thing, I'm so sorry," you should be more like, "Is there anything I can do to help you today?" The person coping with illness is trying to sustain and maintain a quality of life. All your thoughts, suggestions, and offers for help should be in alignment with this. Remember, it is all about quality of life. If you take one thing from this chapter, let it be that. It is not about feeling sorry for someone or coping with sadness. Nope. It is about quality of life, being strong, and being inspirational. That's how we roll.

My love and wishes go to all those dealing with challenges of illness, however mild or severe. I know you can improve your situation somehow. Your struggle has meaning, and you are so appreciated. Thank you and keep up the battle!

CHAPTER ELEVEN
Loss of Pregnancy

Losing a pregnancy is devastating. Most of the time you have invested many weeks of your heart, soul, hopes, dreams, discomforts, thoughts, emotions, and efforts, into a pregnancy. Then for whatever reason, it's gone? Just like that? Often there is no rhyme or reason. Even if there is a clear health reason, it still feels random and unfair. Why you? Why can't you have a healthy baby like others? The questions just keep coming. It's torturous and sad. One of the hardest parts of the whole ordeal is that you often don't feel comfortable being public about it, or grieving too much in the open. You fear people will not think much of it since the baby was never even born. People who have never lost a pregnancy might not fully understand the impact. Too many people out there do not think parents get attached until after birth. Not true. The longer the pregnancy, the more the parents become attached. Also, the more difficult it was to conceive, the sooner parents get attached after conception. By halfway into the pregnancy, many have already started buying supplies and preparing a nursery. Even for those who lose the pregnancy a few weeks in, it is still devastatingly disappointing. They may have been trying to get pregnant for months or years and they thought they FINALLY succeeded. Now all of a sudden it is ripped away from them.

There is a process this loss takes. I mentioned above the anticipation and effort just to get to the point of pregnancy. That in itself may have been a long difficult journey. But then the medical event of losing the baby is very traumatic. I am a male so I cannot completely understand what it is like to have a life in your body one minute, and then the next day it is gone. It seems incomprehensible to me, so I imagine it is extremely traumatic. In addition to the trauma, you have the extreme disappointment and letdown. There is obvious sadness and mourning. Then there are all the doubts of why it happened, and does this mean you cannot carry a child full term. Couples often grieve in different ways, so both of the expectant parents might not even be on the same page of how to handle the incident emotionally. There might be anger, and that anger can be lashed out toward one or both of the partners involved. It is not uncommon for relationships and marriages to end over a failed pregnancy. It is that devastating to all concerned.

This is another example of me unfortunately not having a magic wand that can fix all of this for you. But as with most other serious losses, we can deal with it in such a way that results in a more positive productive outcome, than if we just slumped in a corner. If you do not deal with it correctly, you are at risk of plunging into a deep abyss of depression that can destroy everything around you and steal from you what could be a happy ending if you would give things a chance.

As a male I don't know what it's like to be pregnant, and I cannot fully understand how you feel if you lose the pregnancy. So there is strike one and strike two. But perhaps I can help put things into perspective. Before I go further, let me make the obvious point that although I appear to be speaking to the expectant mother, I fully acknowledge the expectant father is grieving and suffering as well. So any fathers reading this, please know I am not dismissing you. You are included in all that I say, even if the words I am using are directed at the mother. Now let us continue.

First of all, you have suffered a loss. This is a loss that might affect you like any other serious loss. You will be devastated, and you will need to grieve. Do not let anyone make you feel that this is somehow less of a loss. You should feel free to mourn and honor your lost loved one in any way you feel is appropriate and right for you.

Next, you might ask "why?" Well, why does anything

happen? Why do our relatives die? Why do people get into accidents? Why do people get sick and die? Life is full of random tragic events for which we never fully have the answers. We have to accept that life is unpredictable, full of risks, full of tragedies, setbacks, and difficulties. Please do not think this loss is somehow a personal attack against you from God or the universe, or the world. It does not mean you did anything wrong. You might have done everything right. Even when a person does everything right, bad things still happen. Little innocent children who have done nothing wrong get diagnosed with cancer every day. What did they do to deserve that? Nothing.

So please stop blaming yourself for this if you have been. Please view this as any other accidental loss. It is tragic. It does not make the loss easier or justified. But it is a fact of life that random losses happen, even to the best people when it's nobody's fault. Please mourn your loss and respect that it was not your fault, and there might have been nothing you could have done, given what you knew at the time. That leads us to the next step.

Once you have mourned and feel back on solid even ground again, you can do a very objective evaluation of what happened and get some answers. Talk to your doctor. What might have gone wrong? Is there something wrong that you did not know about? Is there something you can do to mitigate the risk of something like this happening again? Look at the situation medically, logically, and objectively. If there are measures you can take to improve your chances next time, then go ahead and work on those.

Decide if you are ready to try this again. If so, when? You must let go of your trauma and fears. You must accept that bad things and losses can happen, and did happen. It does not mean you stop trying and stop living. It just means you realize that things do not always go as planned, and things do not always go well. Very often people fail many times before succeeding. Obviously, you do not want this to be your reality, but you have to accept that it can happen. The best things in life are worth the risk. Just like in love, you have to risk having your heart broken in order to find love. If your heart is broken, you have to risk getting back up off the ground and trying again if you want to experience that love. It is worth the risk and the effort. It's part of life.

So if you choose and are ready, try and try again. Use all the tools at your disposable including your doctor's advice on whether to try, when, and what sort of treatments or pregnancy management is required in your case. Definitely learn from past events and put everything in your favor that you can control. But ultimately, you cannot control everything. That is part of the lesson in all this. Life is a scary journey, and those who are not afraid tend to do the best.

How this story ends is up to you. Perhaps you keep trying and eventually give birth to your beautiful child. Or perhaps you decide to go a different route. Adoption and becoming a stepparent are very beautiful ways to become a parent also. This leads me to the most important point of all this.

Give some consideration as to why you wanted to become a parent in the first place. Most commonly, parents want to leave a legacy of themselves to the world. They want to create little people similar to them that will live on after they are gone. But also, the reason to become a parent is to give love that you have stored up within you. Nobody loves as much as they love their children. So becoming a parent is a way of releasing that love to a little soul. But now consider what I am about to say.

You can do both of those things without having a biological child of your own. You might say, "No you can't because then the child wouldn't be a little me." Well, genetically and physically, maybe not. But regarding mentality, emotionally, values, morals, and everything else that makes a person, the child can be exactly like you. Genetics is not that important actually. What really makes a child

YOUR child is what you give the child for love while raising them to be the best they can be. That child is going to listen to you, learn from you, talk like you, and act like you, even if they are not biologically connected to you. This means you will be raising a child to be similar to you, and you will be leaving a "little you" behind as your legacy. And do I even need to make a case for the fact that you will pour all your love into this child even if it is not biologically yours? What I am saying is that the true reasons you wanted to become a parent can still be fulfilled even if the child ends up not being biologically yours.

I will go one-step beyond that. I will suggest that you do not even need to adopt or take on a child at all. You may choose to give all your love and attention to a niece or nephew. Or maybe you find a way to give your love to children in the form of teaching or counseling. Or maybe you become a mentor to kids who are lacking parental or community support.

However you decide to pursue parenthood, please realize you have more options than you are thinking of, and that they are all valid as long as you are giving a child your love.

Let me say one final thing. Remember that child you lost during pregnancy? Well, they are an angel in spirit looking down upon you and hugging your soul. They may not have been born into a living person, but they felt your anticipation and love anyways. You can know you have collected another angel to comfort you in times of need. That child you lost is still with you. How you take that comfort and move forward is up to you. But please do not give up and stop living. It is time to get back up again and fully engage with life and express your love.

CHAPTER TWELVE
Broken Relationships

You loved them. You trusted them. You depended on them for so much. You thought they would always be there for you. You thought they loved you. But somehow, somewhere along the journey, you both got lost. Or maybe it was just a lie all along. Now you are left feeling broken and incomplete. Alone. Maybe you will never trust again. Maybe you can never love again. Will you ever find anyone else who will love you again?

The pain comes from the betrayal, harsh words, broken trust, but mostly when it's all said and done, it comes from the aloneness. You always had that companion. You also had that security blanket. You had someone you could laugh with and cry with. You had someone to dream with, and make plans with. Your entire future thoughts may have included, and depended upon, this person.

So now you are alone and lost. Everything you thought you believed in, were dreaming of, were planning on, it's all gone now. You are left with nothing of those things now. What you are left with is a broken heart and the inability to ever trust in love again.

It is a life shattering thing, breakups, divorces, endings. A broken relationship can leave you shaken at your foundation. It can leave you wondering about the very existence of romantic love. Or at least leave you wondering about the existence of trust and truth. You wonder how you can ever move beyond this and live again.

You can and you will. But you have to first have some realizations. You have to clearly see WHAT IS instead of what YOU THINK is, and what you WANT it to be. You might THINK the person was perfect until they proved they were not. You might THINK they were the one and only love you could ever have. You might WANT back what you lost, even though it was not ideal. OR, perhaps you have had a total loss in trust, and you THINK you never will, or will never want to, engage in another relationship again, because they will all end the same.

So notice the above paragraph is full of THOUGHTS and ASSUMPTIONS. But what are the FACTS? I do not know the exact circumstances of your situation, so I cannot say specifically. But for example's sake, let us say the FACTS are that you fell in love with a person you enjoyed very much. You were each at a certain place in your life at that time, with certain behaviors, habits, strengths, and weaknesses. The timing and circumstances were perfect enough for you to determine you had found a good match. Life was good and you were happy. You had no reason to believe the relationship would ever change or end.

That last sentence would be your biggest problem. The fact is that relationships always change, and they often end. Also, people change, and so do life circumstances. Everything changes. A universal law is that nothing stays the same forever. So it is only a matter of time before one or both of the people change, or a life circumstance changes, and these things change the relationship. Sometimes this means people are no longer compatible or the relationship is no longer viable.

Regardless of whose fault it is, if a person changes in terms of preferences, personality, behaviors, or habits, they may engage in things that damage the relationship. Or they may start to prefer different types of people. There are many things that can change and go wrong so that they start to distance or detach from the relationship. They may stray to other people outside the relationship that are more in alignment with their new personal changes. Any number of things can happen that will eventually result in something happening that causes a major problem in the relationship. If some major event does not end the relationship, then it might just be a gradual process of detachment and falling out of love.

You can go ahead and blame the other person for whatever they did, or you can blame yourself for what you did, or they can blame you, or you can blame each other. You can chop it up any which way you desire. But the FACT is that people changed, circumstances changed, and therefore the relationship changed. The relationship changed so that eventually it was not viable to one or both people.

Was the person your perfect love? Well maybe they WERE. But they currently ARE NOT because things changed. Thus, if you are lamenting about how you miss them because they were the only one for you, then you might want to reconsider that since the FACT is that they are NO LONGER the perfect one at all. What used to be, and what you want to be, is not the current reality. You must now think in terms of current realities and facts.

I say all this because if you are in pain over a broken relationship, it might be in part because you miss the idea of the relationship, and not the person. It is important you fully realize that you miss the person for who they USED TO BE. You do not miss the person for what they became. You miss how the relationship WAS. You do not miss what the relationship became. What you are missing is a "relationship" that no longer exists, and likely has not existed for a long time. Therefore, there is no point in missing it anymore.

I realize you may have to take a pause and a breath after all that you just read. There is a large shift in thinking to make. However, it is a critical shift in thinking you must make in order to move on from a broken relationship. You have to stop chasing after what WAS. You have to stop wanting something back that changed into something that you truly do not want anymore if you actually thought about it.

For those of you rolling your eyes because you never wanted the person back at all, and you don't want anyone ever again, I will say that this whole exercise in thinking is still important because you still need to release the pain of how you were treated and how things ended. You need to release the pain of the old relationship so that you can at least make a fair and balanced decision about being open to love again, even if you ultimately decide to go solo from now on.

The next realization you need to make is that the end of this relationship does not in any way label you or invalidate you as a person. The other person might be trying to label you with many negative insults. They may be blaming you for things changing. They may be blaming you for things that they themselves are to blame for. They may be trying to brainwash you into thinking you will never find anyone as good as them again, or that you may never find anyone at all again. They may be trying to brainwash you into thinking you are not worthy of anyone's love, including theirs.

OR, maybe YOU are thinking all of those things above about yourself. Maybe your self-esteem has taken a hit and you are brainwashing yourself into thinking you are not worthy of anyone's love. You might be thinking that if they did not love you enough to treat you right, then why would anyone else love you enough to stay by your side. So it works both ways. In fact, most often the greatest damage can be caused by all the "self-talk" of a person who has had their self-esteem damaged to a point that they no longer believe in themselves and don't think they are loveable.

Again, we must live in the reality of facts, and not in what a damaged mind and low self-esteem might try to make you think. You are indeed worthy of love. You are worthy of happiness. Please do not be your worst enemy and try to brainwash yourself into thinking otherwise.

At this point, we have had lots of discussion about what the actual facts and realities are, rather than all the emotional reactions and false thoughts that come from a traumatic situation. The fact is that the relationship stopped being viable for one reason or another. People change, life changes, relationships change, and the universe changes. It worked in the past, but then it stopped working. It ended. It needed to end actually.

I know it is painful. Change is always difficult. It can also be very painful HOW things end and how things change. I understand. I am not dismissing it. However, I need to keep you on a narrow path to victory. Change was inevitable and change happened. Now we get to look forward into the future. You do not need to stay stuck in the past or the present. You do not need to forever lament about what once was, and how you will never have anything again. We must move on. The great news is that you get to re-engineer and design what you want your life to look like now and into the future. You get to consider what you are looking for in future relationships. You get to spend some time working on YOURSELF to become a better and stronger person.

This is where we dry those tears, put away the cookies, and instead go for a walk outside. You get to live again. Most importantly, you get to seek out opportunities and possible relationships that are CURRENTLY in alignment with the person you are, as well as your life and dreams. Remember, the last relationship ended because it was based upon old compatibilities that changed with time. Now you have a chance to build a new relationship that is in alignment with today's version of yourself and your life circumstances.

Be very careful and thoughtful with your choices going forward. Do not fall back into old cycles, behaviors, and choices that no longer serve you in a positive constructive way. This is a new chance for you, so be sure to take full advantage by not making old mistakes inside new opportunities. Very often, it is best to take a moment and be single long enough to get to know yourself again, and become fully aware of what your future desires and preferences truly are.

Some of you might be wondering to yourself if the next relationship will simply run its course and end the same way the last one did. I did say that eventually everything changes. Therefore, will both people change again? Will the next relationship then change and die again? The answer is yes to the first parts. Yes, both people will change. The relationship will change. Does this mean your next relationship will end also? No. It does not mean that.

The length and outcome of any relationship is equal to the ability of both partners to ADJUST to the changes of each other, and to changing life circumstances. Both people must accept that over time things will change. Life will change. Events will happen. Admit it now and brace for it. However, instead of allowing those things to distance you in the future, you can vow to work together so that you can both change and adjust TOGETHER. Accept that you will each be different years from now, and your relationship will be different years from now. But if you can both work closely enough together so that you adjust, change, and accept changes, TOGETHER, then you have a fair chance at the relationship surviving. Relationships that can survive change are the most valuable unbreakable relationships in existence.

Broken relationships can shatter us and make us broken, alone, and sad. But you do not have to stay that way for long. You can get back up, brush yourself off, and move on to a much better future. You are so fortunate to have had experiences that have given you wisdom that you can use to make better choices in the future. You do not need incompatible partners or relationships anymore. Believe in yourself. Do not be labeled or brainwashed by anyone, or by yourself. I don't even know you, yet I know you are worthy of love again. You are worthy of respect. You are worthy of honesty and trust. You deserve another chance at happiness and love. You deserve another chance even if you made mistakes. Nobody is perfect. Everyone makes mistakes. Everyone falls down. Your only job is to get back up again.

CHAPTER THIRTEEN
Toxic People

What causes pain? Toxic people cause pain. Let this be one of the biggest understatements of the book. How many times has your life been damaged, shattered, destroyed, or left in ruins because of toxic people who do not care to even understand how much they have hurt you?

Toxic people manipulate us, control us, tear us down, and hurt us. That's all before lunchtime. Then the rest of the time, their toxicity can actually affect our entire lives, the circumstances surrounding us, and steal our own humanity from us if we do not stop them.

Toxic people can leave us broken, confused, in pain, and lost. We can often feel lost without any direction or way to get back up. They can steal our hope. They can take our self-dignity, self-respect, and self-love. They can take our strength and desire to function in society.

Am I being overly dramatic? Not really. In fact, I could write an entire chapter just on the horrible effects of toxicity and how it makes you feel. I'm sure you could write your own chapter and lists of things toxic people have done to you, and how deeply it has affected you to your very core. So nope, not overly dramatic. In fact, I might be underplaying the devastation by a bit. But we do have to keep things moving along here, right?

We need to establish a baseline for our discussion by going through some of the various types of toxic people. Then we can discuss how to deal with them. I had this same discussion and these explanations in my book *Rising To Greatness*, but it's very important to include all of it in this book as well, so that you have clarity on the different types of people spewing toxicity at you.

SOCIOPATH

There are different official definitions of a Sociopath. It is an actual mental/behavioral disorder. It is associated with the official medical term of ASPD, or Antisocial Personality Disorder. Thus, at its root it is an antisocial disorder. Most people think of Sociopaths as proactively injecting themselves into other's lives to destroy them. This is true in some ways, but the actual medical disorder is the fact that Sociopaths are unable to function socially in a healthy acceptable way. They do not have normal healthy human traits when it comes to socializing with others. An extroverted person with ASPD will start to exhibit Sociopathic traits in a proactive destructive way, as many of us have seen from personal experience and observation.

Here are some common traits of a sociopath:

- Lack of Empathy
- Lack of conscience
- Cold/Callous inner being
- Seemingly charming outer shell
- Manipulator
- Lies constantly to the point of believing their own lies. Could pass a lie detector test.

I am not going to provide an endless list. Obviously, there are countless traits and symptoms of a sociopath. I want to keep it down to the primary traits, so we do not lose focus.

For me personally, I always spot a sociopath by their complete lack of a conscience. This is the telltale sign of a sociopath. They have no conscience because they have no empathy. Due to their antisocial disorder, they are actually incapable of relating to another person on an emotional or empathic level. They do not know how you feel and they do not care. They only care how THEY feel, and about justifying their own feelings. They will make up any lie in order to justify their own feelings or actions. They will manipulate you without conscience to achieve whatever goal they have in mind. They will do this without any regard for your own feelings or well-being. Remember, they have no conscience.

People often fall into the trap of a sociopath because the sociopath can often be very charming on the surface. If you are a person who has emotional weaknesses and vulnerabilities, a sociopath will seek you out and spot you in a second. They will then charm you and stroke your ego and emotions in order to manipulate their way into your life. Once in your life, they will conduct full-on emotional warfare and take everything they want from you until you are destroyed. If you call them out on this, they will make up countless lies as to why they are doing what they are doing. They will manipulate you more in order to get you to accept their behavior. You might believe their lies because you do not detect any regret or guilt from them, so you assume this means they are telling the truth.

A sociopath is usually very polished, smooth, and good at what they do. They can hide lies in plain sight, and they can be amazingly stealthy about hiding other things you will never find. Their manipulations rolled up in lies that you can never penetrate make them very cunning and hard to deal with. But here is how to deal with a sociopath.

1. Identify them as a Sociopath
2. Block them from entering your inner-self

Some of you will think I am being cheeky or funny with my curt solution. I am not. That is literally how to deal with a sociopath. Let me explain. First off, you cannot fix a sociopath. You cannot cure them. You cannot completely stop them from being who they are. So do not try to conquer them. Secondly, there is no way to totally avoid contact with sociopaths unless you move to a remote island on an iceberg. So if you cannot avoid them and you cannot fix them or conquer them, what do you do? Just lock them out. That simple.

Here is an example. Let's say you are forced to have contact with a sociopath. You obviously complete step one, which is to clearly identify and label them as a sociopath. So now you know what they are, how they operate, and what you can expect from them. Then in step 2, you lock them out. You block them from entering your innerself. What I mean by this is that you simply do not buy into any of their nonsense.

Whatever they say to you, just nod your head and say "uh huh." It's that simple. Let's all try it so we know we got it. Ready? Nod your head. Say "uh huh." Awesome, I think you got it. Try it more times if you think you need more practice. But that's it. You do not let them in. Do not believe ANYTHING they say. Do not let their charm engage you. Do not engage with their manipulations. This means do not buy into any compliments they give you since this is normally how it starts. Do not buy into anything.

When you see a sociopath, imagine them as a lion. If you see a lion walking around, do you run up to it and pet it? Do you let it just walk up to you while it licks its lips? No. You walk away. Create distance. If it gets close, you stay silent and make no sudden movements. You just wait for it to leave. So think of a sociopath in that way. I feel bad for using lions as the example because lions are such beautiful creatures. My apologies to lions. But you get my point. The bottom line is that you are not so much dealing with sociopaths as you are identifying them so that you know to put up your walls up.

NARCISSIST

Are we having fun yet? Oh, the fun is just beginning, because now we are going to talk about narcissists. Narcissism is technically referred to as NPD, or Narcissistic Personality Disorder. Narcissism is all about having a total focus on your own self-importance. A narcissist literally thinks they are the center of the universe. Only THEY matter, and that is because they are better and more important than you are. Here are some traits of a narcissist:

- Lack of Empathy
- Exaggerating their own self-importance & superiority
- Consumed with their own appearance, vanity
- Demands constant attention and compliments
- Believe they are more important than you
- Believe you and the entire world exist to serve them and all their needs
- Believe they are never wrong and it is never their fault

The tell-tale sign of a Narcissist for me is someone who thinks they are the center of the universe and nothing is ever their fault. You will almost never hear a narcissist say, "I'm sorry." You are more likely to find Sasquatch than get an apology from a narcissist. Why? Because a narcissist is never wrong, silly. You are the one that is wrong. You owe them an apology. After all, they are more deserving than you are because they are more important than you are. And how dare you be disrespectful by not complimenting them on how wonderful they are 100% of the time. Narcissists are amazing people because they are flawless and wonderful. They can be evil to everyone, but they will still remind you of how kind they are to everyone. If only everyone in the world was as perfect as them, the world would be a great place. In a world full of problems (which the narcissist likely created), they will remind you that they are the one person who is not the problem. Everyone else is the problem. How amazing it must be to live in such delusion, yes?

So how does one deal with such a creature? Here is my two-step plan for dealing with a narcissist:

1. Identify the person as a narcissist
2. Never disagree with them.

Okay well that was easy, wasn't it? Let us go over it in more detail though just to make sure. First thing you will do is clearly identify the person as a narcissist. See them for what they are. The second thing you will do is simply never challenge them. Just agree. If a narcissist tells you that the world is flat and they are the most beautiful creature of all, just respond by nodding your head and saying, "Okay." Let's all try it. Nod your head. Say, "Okay." Very good. I think you got it.

The trick is to engage with narcissists as little as possible. It can never end well. Therefore, just limit your engagement with them. If they say something ridiculous and insulting just say, "Okay." This lack of challenging them disarms them. A narcissist is used to being challenged so they have their knives and baseball bats handy to attack if needed. Therefore, simply do not challenge them. You cannot win. Remember, a narcissist is always right. Plus, even if you won, you would never get an apology anyway, so why bother. Just don't.

GASLIGHTER

Ahhh yes, the Gaslighter. This comes from the term "gas lighting." A Gaslighter is someone who can and will twist anything to their advantage. It does not matter what the subject matter is, a Gaslighter can make it your fault. But a Gaslighter is more than that. A

Gaslighter can victimize and damage you, and STILL make it YOUR fault. Here are some traits of a Gaslighter:

- Accuse you of doing things they themselves did
- Lie
- Deny everything until the end of time
- Harm you and then blame you for it
- Confuse you until you have doubts
- Convince you that you are stupid or crazy even though you are not and they are

The true sign of a Gaslighter is someone who will victimize you, and then blame it on you. A great example of a Gaslighter is someone who cheats on you, but then proceeds to argue that it's your fault they cheated on you. A Gaslighter will twist themselves into a pretzel to confuse you, and show in some convoluted way that they were right and you were wrong. If you call them out on it and prove they were in fact wrong, they will just respond by denying the proven truth and tell you how everything that happens is your fault anyway. A Gaslighter does not believe in reality. If you tell them the world is not flat, they will disagree and accuse you of being too argumentative. Why? Because it's always your fault. Every horrible thing they do to you is always YOUR fault. Whether they cheat on you, lie to you, hurt you, or make a mistake, it will always be your fault they did this. If you challenge them on it, they will have a half dozen tricks up their sleeve to twist it back against you. No matter how horrible a person the Gaslighter is, they will always show you how it is your fault and that you are much more horrible than they are.

How do you deal with such ridiculousness? Two step plan:

1. Identify them as a Gaslighter
2. Don't engage

So, when a Gaslighter is gaslighting, just simply recognize it for what it is. Then simply do not engage with it. When I was a kid, someone once told me to never roll in the mud with a pig, because the pig loves it even if I do not. A Gaslighter loves rolling in the mud. So if you try to engage with them and argue their points with fairness and logic, you will get nowhere, but they will be having a fun time twisting toxicity back at you. Just do not engage in the foolishness.

MENTAL & PHYSICAL ABUSE

If someone is physically abusive to you, leave them. I am not even going to use this as a chance to add content in my book. My books are shorter because there is no need for me to drone on and on about such obvious things. If someone is physically abusive, leave them. They will do it again. They will hurt you, then they will apologize, then they will do again. Rinse and repeat until someone is dead or until you finally leave.

Emotional abuse is common. People are emotionally abusive because of their own issues. It actually has nothing to do with you. The abuser will always blame you and say you "triggered them" and it's your fault for triggering them. Then if they are trying to be honest, they will blame their father or mother for being abusive toward you. But it is usually never their fault to a point where they take full responsibility.

People are abusive toward others usually because others were abusive toward them in the past. Abusers were indeed victims. But it is no excuse for them to be victimizing others. The only cure is for the chain of abuse to be broken. There are two ways to do this as far as your involvement is concerned. The first way is for you to just leave them and stop all contact. That fixes it. But the other way is for the abuser to go into counseling and work on themselves. Abusers can be fixed in the sense that if they take full responsibility for their behavior, AND go into counseling to root out the core cause of their behavior, they can improve with time. People are not born Abusers. They were abused in order to become abusers. So that needs to be identified, isolated, and rooted out. Entire books are written on this.

BULLY

A bully is a jerk who takes out his own insecurities on those he thinks are weaker than him. A bully is not mean because they were born that way. A bully is mean because they are suffering from some issue within themselves. Bullies are often people who were bullied themselves. Bullies are often victims of abuse. The bully takes out their own frustrations and issues on others by treating them in horrible ways, as they themselves have been treated in the past.

The one true mark of a bully is that a bully is always weak inside. Whereas a sociopath or narcissist has the strength of a nuclear arsenal, a bully is nothing but a thin tough exterior covering a fragile weak inner core. Bullies are usually cowards. If they are challenged correctly, they will find a way to save face, back down, and find an easier target.

Therefore, the best way to deal with a bully is to first try avoiding them or diverting attention away to some shiny object in the distance (bullies are not very smart). But if a confrontation is inevitable, the best thing you can do is stand up straight and confront them head-on. A bully fears a strong opponent. If you can appear strong and vicious to them, they will immediately try and find a way to evacuate themselves. Thus, even smarter would be if you "give them an out."

What I used to do with bullies is I would stand up to them. I would show them I was ready to go head-to-head. Then out of the blue, I would say, "You are probably stronger and smarter than me." They would use this as their "out" to back away. This allowed them to "save face" and still feel superior, but allow them to back off without confronting me further, because the truth is that they realized they no longer wanted to confront me when they saw I was willing to stand up to them. They just needed that "out" so they would not look weak and stupid.

Stand up to them with ALL YOUR FORCE, then give them something that makes them think they have won so they can back away. They are not very smart, so some basic psychology tricks work.

BLUFF BULLY

A bluff bully is even more pathetic than a common bully. A bluff bully is one of these gruff people who bark, but have no bite. Not only do they not bite, but often they don't even have any teeth. It is as if they are barking in some delusional way to convince themselves they have power, when in fact they have no power. Bluff bullies are these people you meet who just want to be contrarians. They disagree with everything you say just so they can disagree.

You might say something, and the bluff bully in a loud menacing voice will say, "YOU ARE STUPID, you should go back to school," then they will usually follow that up by laughing as loud as possible. But in truth, they are always the stupid ones. That is why they are bluff bullies. They are engaging in a desperate attempt to make themselves feel smarter and better, even though they know they are pathetic and stupid.

The best way to deal with a bluff bully is to just stare at them. They are not even worth engaging with. That is how pathetic they are. When they are reminded of how pathetic they are by your non-response, because they are too stupid for your time, they will slink off and not bother you.

TROLLS AND IGNORANTS

Trolls and what I call "Ignorants" are just people who enjoy spreading misery as their hobby. These people are miserable themselves. They find some solace in spreading their misery around. These people are a step down from bullies because they usually will not engage face to face. They usually will only engage online, with notes, or messages. They wouldn't dare troll you to your face. These people often act normally in person. The Troll in them only comes out in the semi-anonymity of online social media.

Trolls are very ignorant and have a very low self-esteem. This is why we mostly see trolls going after very successful active people who are heavily involved with projects and social causes. Trolls are insanely jealous of people who live productive meaningful lives. For example, if a twelve year old started their own charity giving away lollipops to children who never get any, the troll would harass the young 12 year old for being controlled by adults into doing such great deeds, and would say that the lollipops are a horrible color. If you point out to the troll that the lollipops come in several different colors, they will just come up with a different angle to hate.

There is absolutely no way to please a troll. They just want to make the rest of the world as miserable as they are. Often they like to disagree even if they agree. They only want to cause frustration and try to drag people down to their level. There is no substance to their behavior and as I said, they often only do this part-time. Get a life I say.

MIXTURES

Keep in mind that any and all of the above toxic types can be combined and mixed together for special blends of gross toxicity. For example, you can commonly face a sociopathic narcissist or a narcissistic sociopath. As the titles would indicate, this is when both types of toxicity are combined.

My personal favorite is a gaslighting narcissistic sociopath. These awful creatures are interesting to observe. They are clear sociopaths, totally delusional with no conscience, who think they are the center of the universe and everyone is wrong about them. They will twist everything back at you to prove they are always right and everything is always your fault. Such a person is constantly telling everyone how wonderful and amazing they are, while victimizing and hurting people, but instantaneously blaming their own hurtful actions on their victims. I think we have all seen this in action, haven't we? Toxicity at its best.

Toxic people put us in pain because they are poison. They can kill our spirit if we buy into their bullshit. Once you truly believe the poison they are spewing, that is when you are truly in trouble. That is why when you believe them, you can lose your sense of who you truly are.

So far in this chapter I have given definitions and tactics for dealing with each. But what we really need to talk about is how you can shift your mentality so that toxic people do not leave you in pain. Dealing with them is one thing, but how does a person protect themselves from them? How does a person not feel sick, sad, or in pain from toxic people?

The answer involves having such a grounded sense of SELF within you, that the toxicity, tricks, and lies that are spewed at you, never seep inside you. Now that you can better identify each one, you need to condition yourself to see them coming a mile away. Size them up immediately and know who and what you are dealing with. Once you can identify and label someone as possibly toxic, you can then raise your shields so that you do not take anything they say seriously or to heart. If it can't get inside you, it can't hurt you inside.

Practice recognizing toxic statements against you, and know they are lies or distortions for the purpose of tearing you down so that you can be controlled or conquered. It's very simple. Where we get into trouble is when we feel beaten down, weak, and we start buying into the bullshit and believing what is being spewed. Then it starts to mentally condition and brainwash us into thinking it is the truth. That is how we get hurt by toxicity. That is what puts us in pain from toxic people. So don't even go there! Identify it right away; recognize it as lies, distortions, and negative tactics. Do not buy into what is being said. Do not let it inside. Remind yourself of who you are, what you stand for, and use logical thinking to remain grounded. Do not be mentally conditioned or brainwashed. All of this might seem obvious, but it's surprising how easily humans can become vulnerable in weak moments and fall victim to the toxicity. Thus, the obvious needs to be said, repeated, and practiced.

Believe in yourself. Do not even engage in toxicity. Do not accept it or fall for it. Block it out. Seeing things clearly for what they are is your best defense against many things. Staying strong against toxic people is one of those examples. Stay vigilant and stay safe! It's a jungle out there!

CHAPTER FOURTEEN
Sexual Assault

I am not going to pretend to know everything about sexual assault. I will not pretend to know how you feel, or how it has affected you, for those who are survivors. But I will try to be helpful in giving you thoughts to consider. Whether you are a woman or man, being a sexual assault survivor means you have experienced something that many others have experienced, BUT in a way that is very unique to you. Everyone's experience, feelings, and trauma is different. Also, everyone processes everything differently. Regardless of the differences, being a survivor of sexual assault changes you and how you look at life. It also leaves you damaged and in pain.

The first thing to consider is that such an event is something that happened TO you. It is not something that you did. That is an important distinction. Even if the other person was your boyfriend or date, it does not shift any blame onto you. Even if you were wearing something suggestive, it does not shift any blame onto you. Even if you sort of intended on possibly having sex, it does not shift any blame onto you. Even if you ended up letting it happen without a fight due to shock or fear, it does not shift any blame onto you. Here is the bottom line. If something happened TO YOU that you did not want, or consent to, then you were sexually assaulted.

Maybe you went on a date and wanted to wear something nice that made you feel sexy. Maybe you even considered that something romantic could happen after the date. That does not excuse your date from forcing something upon you in a way you did not want. Sometimes people who are sexually assaulted have something happen to them that they had considered, but it did not happen in a way they wanted or consented to.

This often means you can become confused as to whether or not you share blame in what happened. The other person might be quick to fully blame you. They might even go further by calling you a whore. You can be easily gas-lighted in such a vulnerable state of mind. It is very common for someone you know to assault you, and then very quickly twist it around to make you feel like it's totally your fault. This makes it so you are victimized twice. The first part is the actual act you did not want, and the second part is that now you have to live with this accusation that it's your fault.

This idea of "fault" or "guilt" is often what causes some of the pain from being a survivor of sexual assault. Therefore, you have to very clearly see what happened and do not accept any gaslighting or blame. You did not DO SOMETHING TO someone. You had something done to you. Be very clear about that in your mind. Don't get it twisted. Again, if something happened to you in a way you did not intend, want, or consent to, then you were assaulted, and THEY are to blame for doing it. Period.

Another part of being a survivor is that you can feel very violated. I do not mean that in simply a sexual way. I mean that YOUR SPACE AND RIGHTS have been violated. You are allowed to have your safe space as a person. That space should never be violated unless you proactively want this and consent to it. When someone violates your space, your rights, your control, or your dignity, they are TAKING SOMETHING from you. They are robbing you of your rights as a human. There are some people who don't understand this. You might say, "He took something from me." The person listening will be waiting for you to explain what he took exactly. Was it a watch, a garment, your phone, jewelry? What did he take from you? They do not understand that what he took from you was much more valuable than a material object. What he took was your freedom, personal space, personal rights, respect, dignity, innocence, or what have you. He has stolen from you what matters most, and you definitely feel like you have been robbed.

Additionally, a major lasting effect resulting in pain is how it changes you. Before the event, you may have been happy go lucky, carefree, relaxed, positive, and "normal." But after the event, you can change into something very different. You may no longer feel free, open, relaxed, happy, "normal," or any number of other things. You now have to live with PTSD and be scared it can happen again. You might have lost confidence as a person that you had before. You might feel you have lost some sort of innocent light within you. You have changed, and not for the better. So you are victimized again by changing into something less than what you were before, in your eyes.

Again, I am not going to pretend to know all the ways it can affect a person. I also know sexual assault can happen woman to man, woman to woman, male to male, and so forth. Please forgive my generalities and specific stereotypical examples as we work through these basic concepts with clarity.

As usual, my suggestion for dealing with traumas like this is to clearly define it for what it is rather than allowing twisted views, gaslighting, or stereotypes to define it. Even if you feel you may have partly participated in the event, you need to accept that it should NOT have happened to you, and you are NOT at blame if something happened to you in a way you did not expect, want, or consent to. I need to spend a moment dissecting that sentence, and you will see why.

For example, let us say someone is threatening you with a weapon or blackmail if you do not have sex with them. In response to this, you consent to have sex with them, because what choice do you really have? So in this example you technically consented. Does this mean you were not sexually assaulted? NO. You definitely were. Why? Because even though you consented (under duress), you did not expect or want it to happen. So don't let the fact that you may have "consented" in a twisted forced way make you feel that you are partly to blame. The perpetrator will certainly try to make you think you consented, and thus it's your fault.

Let's do another example. Let us say your new boyfriend invites you to his apartment. In your mind you are thinking you might want to snuggle with him and kiss. But instead, what happens is he forces himself upon you and has sex with you against your will. Is the fact you "expected" "something romantic" to happen, make it your fault and qualify as consent? NO. Why? Because something happened in a different way you expected, AND you did NOT consent to that kind of sexual activity. You expected kissing and got assaulted instead. More specifically, you consented to kissing and got assaulted instead. You are not to blame. He is.

I am spending this much time explaining all this because it is important for a survivor to fully realize they were not to blame. This means you did nothing wrong. This means you have nothing to be ashamed of. This means you have nothing to hide. This means you should not feel bad about yourself or think you did something wrong.

Fully realize and accept this happened TO YOU. When something happens to us, we take the hit and we try to process what happened, and deal with the aftermath as best we can. It is like being injured. We get injured. We did not ask for it, expect it, want it, or consent to it. It just happens. So what actions do we often take after we are injured? We seek medical or mental health attention as needed. We then rest and heal. We then live our lives wiser and stronger. Do not let an emotional and physical injury of assault beat you. Do not let a sexual assault beat you. You CAN recover physically, emotionally, and spiritually.

You did not ask for this and did not want this. It happened TO you against your wishes. So treat yourself with all the care that is needed to recover from it. This also includes any PTSD or emotional trauma that may have changed you or affected how you live your life. Yes, you might now be wiser and more cautious. That is not a bad thing. But you also need to continue living your life to the fullest without the experience robbing you of that freedom.

If you broke your arm hiking, would you never go hiking again? Of course you would go hiking again. But maybe you would bring a friend next time and watch where you step more carefully. Same with sexual assault. This does not mean you should never date again. It means when you are ready, you can realize what happened in the past is not a guarantee of what will happen again in the future. Maybe just be more cautious and add some safeguards to your routines. But it is important to continue living your life to the fullest when you are healed and ready to move forward.

But what if you feel your dignity, inner peace, and even part of your soul is still missing, having been violated in such an inner personal intimate way? What if you feel they got into your soul and took a part of it with them when they violated your space, trust, and self-dignity as an independent human? I know many survivors feel something very deep inside was taken.

In my opinion, this is giving the perpetrator too much credit. The person who did this to you was not trying to steal your innermost soul. They would not know a soul if it hit them right between the eyes. The person who did this to you was only using your body on a very superficial level. They were not using your soul, inner peace, or your dignity. You CANNOT give up your soul, inner peace, or your dignity if you do not consent to giving up those things. We do sometimes give up those things when we fall in love and give ourselves to the other person. But when we are being assaulted, we are not giving up any of those things. We are simply being physically abused in the moment. This is a very important idea for you to distinguish. Please realize they stole use of your body. They did not steal WHO YOU ARE, or your most inner dignity or soul. You might feel like those precious things were stolen because they feel wounded or injured. But your inner essence and good character is still very much inside you, intact, and under your control. Be very clear to yourself that you still have them, even if they are temporarily injured. The moment you think they stole those most inner treasures, is the moment you give the perpetrator more credit than they deserve, and you give them more than what they were seeking. They were only seeking temporary use of your body. They were not able to get anything else because you never consented to giving up anything else.

Again, I know my generalizations do not cover every possibility, such as molestation from a relative, or workplace assault, and so forth. But my concepts can still be used. There is no reason for you to feel defeated, guilty, scared, or less of a person due to being a survivor of sexual abuse. The healing process is recognizing that you were injured without expecting it, wanting it, or consenting to it. You must now heal from this injury and violation of your space and rights. You then move forward with the wisdom and strength you gained from the experience and healing process.

We do not become less of a person. We become a better stronger person.

CHAPTER FIFTEEN
Abuse

Abuse. The systematic tearing down of a person for the purpose of either controlling them or projecting one's pain onto another person for self-gratification. The key phrase is "systematic tearing down of a person." This can be done psychologically or physically, or both.

If you have suffered abuse, your self-esteem is likely shredded, the abuser has tried to make you feel like a piece of trash, and you are probably traumatized by the entire experience even if you managed to remove yourself.

The abuser will bully you, insult you, and gaslight you. An abuser will always treat you like garbage, but then twist things to make it look like it's your fault. An abuser will make you feel worthless, stupid, and always at fault. The abuser uses these tactics on an on-going basis so that you are brainwashed into believing that you really are worthless, and it really is your fault. Once the abuser has you in this frame of mind, they CONTROL you 100%. They will remind you that you are stupid and you should listen to them, believe what they say, and do whatever they tell you because they are superior and you are nothing. They will condition you to seek their approval and validation. They will give you just barely enough encouragement so that you keep begging them for more scraps of validation. Eventually, they make you feel like you cannot live without them. So you stay with them. You put up with it. You put up with it because you feel you are not strong enough or good enough to survive without them. They have succeeded in brainwashing you into believing you are nothing and that they are superior.

Once you get to this point, you of course feel inferior, weak, and of little value as a person. This equals pain. This is the REAL pain. Yes, their insults and attacks are painful. But those are not nearly as painful as how you feel as a person, who has been totally broken down to nothing.

You might not love yourself anymore. Why would you love yourself if the abuser has brainwashed you into thinking you are not worthy of love? They say that maybe if you were a better person, you would be worthy of love. Maybe if you listen to everything they say, and do everything they tell you to do, you will possibly be slightly more worthy of love. But you see, you never quite get there. However, the abuser will "encourage" you to keep trying. They will give you tiny amounts of validation so that you keep trying for more. But they will never give you enough so that you feel any sense empowerment. Your empowerment is their enemy.

All of this can go on for years. You can lose your sense of SELF and your sense of personal identity. You forget what happiness is. You feel no love for yourself. You feel too weak to even try anything different. You are tired, depressed, beaten down, sad, and hopeless. You might even feel like dying. You cry when nobody will see you, and you cry inside when people can see you. You try to act like a normal healthy person in public, but inside you are dead, scared, and hopeless. You are trapped in hell.

Let's release you from hell, shall we? Whether you are currently suffering from abuse, or you are still recovering from abuse, the principles we will discuss apply. I promise that you deserve more than the hell you are living. I promise you have more value as a person than you have been made to believe. I promise things can get better.

The first step is realizing that you have been brainwashed into believing something that is not real. You might believe you are weaker or lesser of a person. You might have a low self-esteem. You might not love yourself because you feel deep down you must not be worthy. If the abuser did not find you worthy of love, then maybe it's because you are not worthy? ALL OF THAT IS A LIE. LIES!

Let's look at something. A child is born. Every child is born with human traits and is seeking love. Every human is seeking love. If a child is nurtured in a safe normal environment, they naturally love and receive love. They grow up learning their strengths and weaknesses. I assure you that IS how you started out.

However, what can often happen is that at some point that human development is interfered with. Whether it be in childhood or later in adulthood, the child of love and balanced behavior (strengths and weaknesses), can be conditioned (brainwashed) into thinking artificial or false facts and realities. If a person tells you that you are stupid every day for months, you will likely end up believing that you are stupid. Even if you are a genius, you will think you are stupid because you were brainwashed through systematic conditioning, or in other words, systematic abuse.

Once you are brainwashed to think those false realities, you are vulnerable to attack and being controlled by abusers. My point is that you need to logically recognize that you have been systematically brainwashed to feel like less of a person. It is a false reality. So realize you have been programmed with a false reality. You need to now reject that false reality. Think of EVERYTHING the abuser told you. Know that it is all a lie. Even the good things the abuser told you were only said in order to validate you just enough to keep controlling you. Thus, you need to process everything the abuser told you, and reject it as false.

Deprogramming yourself from all of the abuser's falsehoods only gets you back to zero. Once at zero, you might still feel lost. You might ask yourself, "Well if I am not all the things the abuser said, then what am I?" The human mind will always look for ways to fill a vacuum. So even if you throw the bad things out, your mind will immediately need to fill that space with something else. Therefore, be aware of this and be careful not to refill your mind with different bad things.

Instead, fill your mind with positive things. The one weapon and "go-to" tool you can always use is love. Think of things you love doing, love thinking about, or those people you love or love helping. Think of what you love about yourself. I know for some that might be difficult at first. If you have been conditioned to think there is nothing loveable about you, then how can you think of something you love about yourself, right? But we just got rid of all the false programming. So think simply for a minute. I know something. Yes, I might not know you that well, but I still know something loveable about you. You are a survivor. You can take abuse and still survive. You have been programmed to think you are weak. But that was a lie. In actuality, you are strong. Only the strong can endure abuse for long periods of time. I love that you are a survivor. I love that you are strong enough to endure your abuser. I love that you have the intelligence and desire to read this book in order to heal yourself. There is plenty to love about you.

Already we are filling the vacuum with more positive and TRUE facts and realities. Keep doing that. Think of more things. Make a list and take notes if you want. Remind yourself often of what is loveable and good about yourself. Remember, you were conditioned with bad things over a period of time. Brainwashing does not happen overnight. It happens through constant and systematic conditioning (abuse) over time. So you also need to condition yourself with the good things systematically over time. Therefore, have some patience. Realize you need to keep reminding yourself of the good things systematically over time.

If you are reconditioning your thoughts about yourself, and you still feel pain from the abuse, why is this? If you still feel pain, it is likely because you still believe in some of the abusive lies. At this point, the pain is equal to the belief in negative falsehoods. You might be following my suggestions and making progress, but deep down you still feel like less of a person or less worthy? Perhaps you still feel less worthy of love?

The reason for this is there must be a CORE ISSUE that needs to be resolved. Let us say for example that an abuser throws ten insults at you. Perhaps some of them are superficial and you quickly realize they are false. Thus, you are able to dismiss it more easily during your reconditioning. However, there might be one of the insults that hits too close to home. Perhaps you feel it has some truth to it, therefore you cannot dismiss it as easily as the others. You need to identify THIS core issue.

I cannot go over every potential core issue in this book. But examples might be that you made a mistake in your life and that mistake is being used against you. Perhaps it is a physical weight or appearance issue. Perhaps it is a behavioral problem or addiction. The point is that there might be something that you actually feel IS your fault. THIS is the core issue that the abuser threw at you that you can't dismiss as a false fact or reality. So since it is not false in your own mind (even if it is false), it becomes a remaining reason why you still feel like less of a person and less worthy of love.

You need to find and identify those core issues you seem unable to discard. Then realize this: NOBODY IS PERFECT. Every human is flawed. Every human makes mistakes. Every human has behavior problems and issues. Every human has weaknesses. FACT. So now, YOU need to stop abusing YOURSELF with any weakness or issue you may THINK you have. Having a weakness is not justification for thinking less of yourself or not loving yourself. Having a weakness means you are human like everyone else, and you can put it on your list of things to work on and improve.

Let me state it again more clearly. Any true weakness you have is not justification or reason for being less worthy as a person or unlovable. Weaknesses are only justification for things to improve upon. A healthy worthy loveable person has weaknesses. They can work to improve upon them. So when you identify any core issues that you were unable to dismiss as a false fact, just set it aside as a weakness that needs work. You are still worthy and loveable. You need to start thinking to yourself, "Despite my weakness of (insert weakness), I am still worthy and loveable."

Through all of your efforts, you have discarded the false facts, you have filled the vacuum with true positive facts, and you have identified any remaining core issues and set them aside as items to work on, realizing you are still worthy and loveable despite them.

At this point, you have to be very careful with whom you surround yourself. If you surround yourself with other abusers, you can still easily fall victim again. Therefore, be very aware of who you are interacting with. Become very aware of anyone who says or does things that make you feel less of a person. If you see or feel that, you need to immediately realize THAT is the beginning stages of another cycle of abuse. Remove yourself from that person and environment. Put yourself in environments filled with love, support, and encouragement.

Remember, the point of this book is to heal. Are you healing from abuse? If you are, then keep going with the process of long-term reconditioning. If you still feel pain from abuse, that means you still have core issues that need to be identified and resolved. Rinse and repeat the process. A good counselor can be very helpful in identifying these core issues so that you can set them aside and resolve them.

You are deserving of love. You are a person capable of good things. You are capable of surviving abuse. You are capable of recovering, reconditioning, and healing.

CHAPTER SIXTEEN
Self-Esteem

Self-esteem is an issue with which many people struggle. There might be nagging reasons in the back of your mind or the pit of your stomach as to why you do not feel at your best. You may not want to be noticed or even socialize at all. You might be afraid to speak your mind or defend your positions. You might not want people to even look at you. You might not want to even look at yourself. Some people actually remove all their mirrors from their home. Or perhaps you just feel unworthy of love, attention, and respect. Maybe you feel you are not of great value, or that you are not valued by others.

These feelings can leave us really depressed, and definitely hamper us from living our lives to the fullest, and experiencing joy. Sometimes these feelings of depression can actually lead to very destructive behaviors such as eating disorders or social anxieties. Some people get to the point where they will not even leave their home anymore. Self-esteem is no longer an optional feature we teach children through sports and other activities. Self-esteem is something we all must have healthy doses of or we cannot live our lives effectively. A poor self-esteem leaves us in pain, and we suffer. That is why we are discussing it here.

I know a lot of you feel a damaged self-esteem on some level. It might have a root that is more physical, or it might be more mental or emotional in nature. Or more precisely, it is mental, which is then also manifested in a physical way through various disorders. The struggle is real and we have to address it.

How did we get this way? How did we end up with a damaged self-esteem? Well it usually starts in childhood. Humans have this notion that they must be equal or better when compared to others. Even worse, is that society gets to set the definitions and standards of what is "better." Society decides how skinny is too skinny, and how skinny is "just right." Society decides what your face should ideally look like, as well as how your hair should be, your characteristics, and everything else. Human society builds that set of standards from which all humans are to be compared and judged.

Once we have our set of standards telling us what is "good" and "not as good," we then let other children, parents, and members of society, persecute us based upon the standards we do not meet. So if the standard is to be a certain body type, of not too big and not too small, those around us will judge how well we meet the standards, and at what level we should be persecuted for not meeting the ideal standards.

Do I need to remind you these "ideal standards" are a false artificial guide? Who created you? Whether your answer is something like "God" or "nature," the fact is that you were created perfectly the way you were supposed to be created. Clearly, our creator wanted a huge variety of characteristics in humans.

I have been obsessing over physical qualities such as weight and general appearance in my explanations above. These standards extend into personality traits as well. For example, the standard set by society commonly indicates a person needs to be very outgoing, well mannered toward authority, academic, and athletic. So if you are a quiet introverted person who thinks outside the box and prefers reading instead of sports, then you don't fit the mold, and are often made to feel uncomfortable for your personality traits. This set of societal standards applies to the physical as well as to personality traits, behaviors, and preferences. Do we even need to get into sexuality and other such things? No, I think you get the point. We are all judged upon a very ridiculous artificial set of societal standards we had no say in creating.

At a very early age we are observed, examined, compared, and judged by everyone around us. If there are any areas for which we fall outside the normal standard boundaries, we are then persecuted for that particular "offense." People make fun of us for our particular differences and traits that differ from the artificial societal standards. Pretty much everyone goes through this persecution, because it is rare for any one person to fit inside all the normal standards. So whether you were judged as too skinny, too fat, too short, too tall, too smart, too stupid, too quiet, too loud, too beautiful, too ugly, or so on and so forth, you have likely been persecuted for something.

What does this have to do with self-esteem? Well, once you begin to be persecuted for one or more particular traits, the emotional damage begins. Emotional damage occurs with the systematic and ongoing bullying, which targets specific things. It is a form of brainwashing. After you are persecuted for a long enough period of time, you begin to actually believe what the bullies are saying to you.

If you have enough people telling you that you are "too fat" or "too quiet," you will eventually come to believe you are "too fat" and "too quiet." You will process this information as factual evidence of you being "below standard," dysfunctional, broken, or bad. Basically, others start labeling you as being less than desirable, and not long after that, you actually believe you are less desirable. This is the exact moment your self-esteem is damaged.

At that point, you would feel bad about yourself because you truly believe you are less desirable. Your proof is the fact that all these other people have been pointing out that you are less desirable. The next logical step your psyche takes is to try and hide your below standard trait. So if you have a personality trait you are hiding, you will avoid social settings and keep your thoughts to yourself. If you have a physical trait deemed as below standard, then you will try to hide it, or you will just avoid being seen by anyone at all.

Any way you slice it, you are now living your life in a way where you are trying to compensate for your persecuted trait by doing things or not doing things. It starts to control your life. Plus, you have to live in constant fear of society still persecuting you on an on-going basis. It wasn't bad enough that you had to deal with a bunch of playground brats in elementary school, but you STILL have to put up with random strangers making comments as an adult. It never ends. This is painful. So this is where we often develop various phobias and social disorders in response to the trauma of persecution. Not only do we have to worry about everything already mentioned, but now we have to deal with our newly acquired social disorders as well.

The bottom line of all this is that we no longer live our lives to the fullest. We are no longer living to be happy and productive. We are just living in pain and suffering from our damaged self-esteem. This holds us back from everything. It holds us back from doing things in life we would love to do. It holds us back from pursuing career goals more aggressively. It holds us back from going up to the person who we think is cute and having conversation. It holds us back from leaving our house or being social at all. It holds us back from engaging in self-care, exercise, intellectual pursuits, and just taking care of ourselves in general. Due to a damaged self-esteem, we basically don't live our lives as we should. A poor self-esteem is like being in a candy store, but your feet are glued to the floor. You cannot move. You cannot get what you want. So why bother being in a candy store if you can't move and get what you want? That is the point. A poor self-esteem makes us question why we are even bothering to try at all. It makes us question why we should even live.

A false narrative of artificially twisted bullshit, which is then manifested into a form of societal bullying, is what hurt us. This caused us mental trauma, which caused more serious mental anxieties. This then caused us to stop living our lives and cry inside ourselves with pain. This torture is so meaningless and needless. It is a societal self-inflicted wound that never had to happen. You were born perfect, how God and nature intended. This nightmare string of events never needed to happen. But yet, here we are.

So what do we do now? We have to step out of this false narrative. We have to declare to ourselves that the artificial societal standards are invalid. If you take away one thing from this book, please take away the idea that all persecution, bullying, insults, and abuse, is powerless against you as long as you do not believe in it. All of this toxicity only works against you if you are successfully brainwashed into believing it is true. If you can bring your self-empowerment and sense of self to a level where you cannot be brainwashed, then you will be immune from these toxic forces. Just simply do not believe in the bullshit, and you are cured.

Therefore, you need to reprogram yourself so that you understand that all humans are created differently for a divine or natural reason. Diversity is healthy. Your traits are varied. Some of you might like yourself, and some of you do not. If you do not like some of your traits, then you have the personal freedom to change them. But that is YOUR choice. Do NOT let society make the choice for you. Only change if you prefer and choose to change. Otherwise, you are fine the way you are.

Also, start focusing more on your strengths. If you have what YOU view as a physical weakness, you can compensate for that by showing your personality strengths. Maybe you are not athletic, but you are intellectual or smart. Maybe you are not exactly a genius, but you are funny and nice. Maybe you are short, but you are charming. To be very honest with you, I do not really feel you should be forced to even compensate for things at all. This in a way indirectly justifies or gives credence to the societal standards. However, I am suggesting this method of compensation is a way of dealing with poor self-esteem issues. We engage with coping mechanisms and strategies that work to better us. I believe this is one way to do it, even if it is not ideal.

But you need to really do the work within yourself so that you do not even feel a need to compensate. You need to believe in yourself. You need to know your strengths and weaknesses so that you are comfortable with yourself for how you are. There is no need for compensation within yourself once you are more comfortable with yourself. You have to undo all the brainwashing that made you actually believe that you are somehow inferior in certain ways.

This is why I suggest believing it inside, but then also using your strengths to gain confidence in fully engaging with life. Don't be shy. Remember, everyone is "too" something. So whomever you are nervous to deal with also has something they are nursing as "below standard." Do not be intimidated by anyone. Celebrate the full you. Celebrate all your diverse traits. Own the traits that some think are not the normal standard, in addition to parading the traits that most would admire.

Deep inside, you need to admire all of your traits that make you unique and special. You can choose to alter some traits that you yourself are not fond of. You can choose to accentuate the traits that you yourself are particularly proud of. You are in control, not society.

A good self-esteem is when you are comfortable with yourself. Are you comfortable with yourself? Consider that question after reading everything we have been discussing. I am hoping some things you were not comfortable with before, you might decide you are going to become comfortable with now, because they are natural traits that make you unique and wonderful in a special human way. However, if there are some traits you are still not comfortable with, please ask yourself why. Is it because the persecution and brainwashing was so intense that you will need much more self-work before you are comfortable? Or is it because you sincerely do not like certain traits and you wish you could change them? Consider those questions carefully. De-program the brainwashing on the items you can accept about yourself. Then take actions to change the items that you actually want to change from your own choice.

The act of taking action to change, is in itself, very uplifting for a person's self-esteem. Do not be afraid to change things that would make you feel more comfortable about yourself. Maybe you did not do this before because you felt beaten down and everything just seemed too overwhelming. Maybe you kind of gave up. Maybe this caused you to give up on life.

It is time to change that. Do not give up on life. Make the effort to restore your self-esteem to a healthy level. Make the effort to change traits you want improved. You do not need to be a victim of our toxic society and their artificial standards. You do not need to buy into the societal persecution of what you should be or not be. You do not need to live with all the brainwashing that has been forced upon you over the years. The societal bullying that damaged your self-esteem can be reversed if you reprogram yourself to no longer buy into the bullshit being forced upon you.

I understand many of you have very deep wounds. I talk about "society," but many of your self-esteem wounds may have been inflicted by parents, romantic partners, or other specific people. I know it is not just about "society." But the principles of how to handle all of this are the same. It is important to realize you were created into a diverse unique being on purpose, and that you can shed all the brainwashing and bullying that caused your mental trauma. You can also make a personal choice to change some traits you do not like. You can seize control over your self-esteem. This allows you to seize control of your life. You can do it! You are worthy of love, happiness, and all the wonderful things life has to offer. Do not ever believe anyone who tells you otherwise.

CHAPTER SEVENTEEN
Estrangement

Being estranged from family and close friends can be a major issue and a source of great pain. We are going to define estrangement as a break in the relationship with a family member or close friend. A break in the relationship meaning communication and contact has stopped.

Some people do not understand the difference between estrangement and a traditional relationship that has ended. When your feelings or circumstances meet a brick wall or impasse with romantic partners or friends, there is a decision made to end the relationship. The relationship no longer works and is dead. One or both parties believe that moving on in different directions is the action of choice. Usually an ended relationship means you no longer love the person as you did, or the relationship is toxic and needs to end.

Estrangement is different because it usually involves a family member or close friend that you cannot just "end" the relationship with and never see them again. In most realities, we cannot simply end a relationship with a parent or child and forget about them as if they never existed. In some way, that person is stuck in your life whether you like it or not. You might always love them as your parent or child, even if you can't stand them, or feel they have been cruel toward you. Estrangement is for those situations where you really cannot erase them from your life as you can with romantic relationships.

Estrangement is painful because it involves people you thought would always have your back and that you could trust, because the bond was beyond the normal relationship bond. A parent/child bond is such that there is a love and trust that exists even if you do not get along well with that person. Thus, an estrangement from them is losing family, which is like losing a part of yourself.

Family is precious even if you don't like being around them all the time. My proof of this is all those family holiday get-togethers that you dread, but still participate in. You know for certain there will be issues and hard feelings at these family gatherings, yet deep inside you "want" to connect with your family still, even if it will be twisted. Humans by nature have a natural need for family connections. Family are people who have to like you even if they hate you. Well sort of. Maybe.

You can see I am leaving estrangement open to important people in your life, but it's hard to discuss estrangement without assuming it is parent/child or between siblings. But yes, it can also be with best friends who have known each other their entire lives, or other extended family members for which there was a strong bond in the past. For purposes of example, we will stick with the most common and obvious, that being the parent/child relationship.

The pain of estrangement between parent/child stems from the fact that the parent feels they loved their child and gave them everything, and yet the child might not appreciate, respect, consider, or show any love toward the parent. Obviously, this is extremely painful and insulting to the parent. Hard feelings develop and there is a cut in contact and communications.

Conversely, a child might feel that the parent has always persecuted them and they never received what they wanted or needed from that parent. Maybe they never received the recognition, time, attention, respect, loyalty, and love they felt they needed, wanted, and deserved. They are tired of feeling ignored or abused by the parent. Hard feelings develop and there is a cut in contact and communications.

So those are common examples of both sides. That leads us to the next point. There are always two sides to every story. The parent has valid points and the child has valid points. Both are hurt. Yes, the blame may be more on one side than the other. But pain resides on both sides. If you cannot recognize this, then your estrangement has no chance of ending. You must at some point realize that both sides are hurting and have valid reasons, at least in THEIR minds.

The first order of business in sorting through an estrangement is to examine the reasons for it. Did it start from a stupid argument that nobody remembers? Did it start from one person making a horrible mistake? Did it start from apathy of both parties just not wanting to connect? Did it start because one side broke off all contact for whatever reason? Did it start because there was abuse or toxicity from one or both parties? Why did it start? Notice I am not using the word blame. I am just looking for you to identify why it started.

The reason it started will determine the next step. For example, if estrangement started from a stupid argument or hard feelings from something that has long washed under the bridge, then you need to recognize that the estrangement is simply stupid and needless. However, if the estrangement started from abuse and toxicity, then you may want to consider if you want to re-engage at all if the person has not changed.

Again, I did not use the word blame. I was just asking you to determine if the estrangement should be ended or continued. This is an important juncture and determines your actions and behaviors going forward. This also determines your level of acceptance for the situation that exists.

If you determine the estrangement should continue because the person was and still would be toxic, abusive, or destructive to you, then you need to find peace within your estrangement. You might feel pain from the estrangement because you "miss" them. But you need to realize that what you are missing is some perfect ideal or past circumstance that does not exist in today's reality. So if it does not exist, then you should not miss it. Instead, you need to let it go as you would a broken marriage or death. It was important and special at points in the past, but it has gone now. So you need to give it love for what it WAS, but give it no more energy for what it IS presently.

If you determine the estrangement should end, then that means one thing. YOU must be the one to make the first move. Notice how I still did not mention blame. It is not relevant. Also, if you are waiting for the other person to make the first move, you will continue to suffer from the estrangement. They are likely not reading this chapter, you are. You need to be the bigger person and take action to end it. You are not ending it because you are sorry for something you did or feel you did something wrong. You are not admitting to anything. You are simply trying to end your pain by resolving the estrangement one way or another. That is what this is about, right? We need to end our pain. With estrangement, we can only end our pain by resolving it, whichever way it needs to be done.

So if you have decided to try and end it, you will make the first move. Small moves are usually the best for both parties. You don't need to stick your neck all the way out there. Maybe a simple message asking how they have been. Maybe ask about a mutual person or concern. Ask them about something you heard they did or happened to them. Reach out in some way. If they have been waiting and wanting for you to reach out, they will likely respond in some reasonable time, although maybe not immediately. If they do not respond at all, it might be they are preferring to continue the estrangement. In that case, you have to realize they are not the person they once were, and would not be a loving support in your life anyway. So again, I ask, "What are you missing?"

During these initial contacts, you should avoid any mention of blame unless you feel you have something to apologize for. If you feel to apologize for something, do so. Make it short and to the point. Do not re-litigate the entire situation. Instead, just mention how so much time has passed, life has changed, your outlook has changed, and you have missed them and you are sorry for what happened that hurt them. See, just like that.

Then you want to quickly MOVE ON. Keep it positive and keep it looking forward. No blame and no re-litigating. Instead, engage in topics that would be of interest to both of you presently. You are not really looking to turn the clock back and try to "fix" everything that happened. The best method is really to acknowledge the past pain, but then focus on the potential of today and tomorrow. You are starting new. You are not starting old and trying to resume. You need to likely brush the old under the rug and start new from your present position.

Do not focus on how they have not changed, or how they still have traits you dislike. Rather, focus on the traits you missed the most and enjoy. Focus on any new traits you see have developed during the time you were estranged. Look at them as a new person. Be sure to notice any changes and appreciate them. Don't step into the pile of dog doo, that is, being the old traits and issues that you know will result in an argument or bad feelings. This time around, you will avoid those issues rather than fighting over them. You are smarter and wiser now. Embrace things you love, and simply avoid things you dislike. Only teenagers fight every fight. Adults know it is smarter to avoid almost all fights. Yes, I know when it comes to parent/child relationships, we all get transported back in time and feel like children again with our parents. Also, parents always look at their child as a child, regardless of age. But you need to resist this temptation to fight every fight. It's not easy. I often fail at that and perhaps many of you do as well. But it truly is the best way forward to avoid the fights, and instead focus on areas of agreement and enjoyment.

Practice makes perfect. Remember that everyone is in pain about something, including the person you are, or were, estranged from. Have some compassion for that pain. Try to spot the areas of appreciation and enjoyment. Focus on those. Compassion, patience, and love. Always the best policies. Whatever your decision is regarding your estrangements, make them with wisdom, compassion, patience, and love for both yourself and for them.

CHAPTER EIGHTEEN
Toxic World

Many people become upset and in pain as they watch the world around them become more toxic and seemingly self-destructive. It is hard to maintain a sense of peace and happiness when everything around you is toxic and declining into what appears to be a hopeless abyss. World events outside of a person's personal bubble, you would think would not evoke such despair and pain. Yet they do.

Why is this? How can a person with a decent happy life be in pain from the toxic world around them? The answer, I believe, can be summed up in two words. Empathy and Conscience. A person who is particularly empathetic and has a strong social conscience, actually FEELS the pain of the people and Earth around them.

The best example I can come up with, which some might find offensive, and is exactly why it's the best example I can come up with, is involving animal abuse. Let's say you own a dog and you take great care of your dog. You have a great home, great career, great social life, and you are actually very happy with your life and how things are going with your life. You also have a dog that is wonderful, healthy, and very well taken care of. So you should be delighted with life and nothing can rain on your parade. However, now let's say that your neighbors around you also have dogs, but you see them chained up outside at all times, with no attention, no care, and looking scared and hungry. You are surrounded by suffering dogs from abusive owners. Just the sight of this, and thought of this, is enough to put many people into a very upsetting deep depression. Their inner perfect world means nothing if they are surrounded by a toxic world.

So basically, it does not matter how wonderful your own personal world is. If the world around you is toxic, it can easily bring you down to a very low level of despair, even though your personal world is great. A toxic world is responsible for ruining what would otherwise be very fine lives. It is especially frustrating because it's very difficult, even on a good day, for someone to create happiness in their own world. So think of the frustration of succeeding within your own world, only to end up miserable in the end, because of the toxic world around you.

What is a person to do? You turn on the news and see nothing but pain and destruction. Are you supposed to ignore it? Pretend it does not exist? Never turn on the TV? Hide inside within your hidden bubble for the rest of your life? What's the answer?

My normal answer for such things usually involves directly facing it. Face your fears. Face your problems. Face the truth of yourself. Face the tasks in front of you. I am all about facing up to what is trying to defeat you. I think this should be no different. You need to face reality. You need to face the toxicity. Face the toxic world around you. But there is one twist to this strategy.

Usually we face things in our life so we can square off against them and defeat them. In the case of a toxic world, we cannot defeat the world. So the twist to our strategy is that we must accept our limitations in how we face off against this challenge. We will not defeat the world, and we will not rid the world of toxicity. We cannot solve world hunger and world peace on our own. But what we can do is BE THE CHANGE. We can acknowledge the problems around us, while we remain very aware of our own personal values.

If you think the world is too cruel, then go out into the world and be kind. If nobody shows kindness anymore, go out in the world and show kindness. If nobody listens to other opinions anymore, then go out and be sure to show patience in listening to other opinions. If everyone is greedy and lacking in compassion, then go out and make an effort to be generous and show compassion. Be the change you want to see. Be the values you think are missing.

You cannot single handedly solve all the world's problems. But you can be part of the solution. I do not mean for any of this to sound obvious or clichéd, although to some of you it might. It is in this book because living in a toxic world is very painful for many people. We are here to try and free ourselves from pain. So I have no problem sounding clichéd or obvious if this is what some people need to hear, realize, or see further validation of before they actually adopt it into action.

Facing a toxic world means accepting there is a toxic world you cannot fix. It also means being part of the solution, even though your actions alone won't fix it. It actually takes a lot of courage and conviction to work at something when you know you will not succeed with your efforts alone. Therefore, it is not about succeeding. It is about living your own values. It is about doing the right thing. It is about self-empowerment. When we are self-empowered enough that we live our own values and take our own actions, even though we know the victory won't come tomorrow, we still feel that we are living up to our own standards and morals. We are being the change. We are making a difference. We are being the example for others to notice and follow. We are being encouraging to others who are doing the same as we are. We are living and acting in a way to keep the dream alive that someday things will be better. We do this for the love we have of our children, humanity, and Mother Earth. We do it for love. Anytime you do something for love, it is always the right thing.

So yes, you might live in a toxic world. Yes, it is depressing. But you do not have to be depressed. In fact, you can UPLIFT yourself by being "the change" and part of the solution. You can uplift yourself by showing love to your cause. You can uplift yourself by knowing you are proactively living up to your own morals and values. Do not be in pain. Be inspired.

CHAPTER NINETEEN
Anger

Most people can agree that anger is a major issue that can keep us in pain for a long time. Some people have such horrible anger issues, that they cannot function without some kind of regular outburst. We need to address anger as a major reason many people cannot let go of things, and remain tortured and in pain for years.

Oh no, did I just give away the entire key to the chapter in the first paragraph? "Many people can't let go of things." Not letting go of things is a theme that comes up in many issues that leave us in pain. Anger is one of them. But let us take a more in-depth look at anger.

What is anger exactly? Anger is basically a very intense frustration in response to something that happens to us or is said to us. Anger is such a classic human trait. For you aliens out there, it is not as much of an issue because you all think so logically. But for humans, anger is a common natural response to things we think are unfair or harmful to our agenda in life. I guess the best way to look at this, might be to use an example.

Let's say we are minding our own business and living our lives as best we can within a difficult world. We have been saving money for something we wanted, but then we get a letter in the mail informing us that our rent is increasing. Our brain in less than one second figures out that this rent increase just wiped out the extra money we have been able to save for something we wanted. At the exact same time our brain has calculated this, we also become angry instantaneously. What are we angry at? Are we angry we have to pay rent? No, we know we have to pay rent. Are we angry that there are rent increases? Yes and no. We are angry about THIS rent increase and increases imposed upon us personally, but we also fully realize there WILL BE rent increases. So if we knew there would be rent increases from time to time, then why are we so angry about THIS rent increase? The answer is that THIS rent increase is taking away our ability to get something we really wanted. THAT makes us angry. We are actually angry because we can no longer get something we wanted with the extra money we were able to save. We are basically experiencing an adult tantrum. Was this event our fault? Nope. The fact it was not our fault and not our doing might in fact make us even more angry.

Now let's look at a second example. Same as in the first example, we are saving our money for something we want. However, one day we are moving things around in the living room and we end up accidently dropping the TV on the floor and breaking it. Wow, are we angry! Why are we angry? We are angry because we just broke something expensive. Our initial thought might be that we are angry with ourselves for being stupid and reckless. OR, in some cases, a person is just angry because the TV broke. Yes, they may skip the step of blaming themselves. They might be angry the TV was not strong enough to withstand a drop. Was this our fault? Yes. Does this make us more angry or less angry? Well, some people will be less angry because at least it was not unfair. At least they have control over it. But others will be more angry because it was their own actions that broke it. Some will become more angry if the blame can be placed upon them. People vary on how they react to such an event. But either way, everyone would be angry about this incident.

I do not want to get too lost in the weeds with these examples. I just wanted to point out that anger is an automatic response people have when something bad happens to them. I also wanted to point out that the reason people get angry, and what exactly they are angry at, will differ from person to person, even in the exact same incident experienced by many people.

However, they all have one thing in common. The anger is a natural automatic response, and the anger has to be directed at something. Something or someone must be at fault when anger is involved. Who or what is to blame? So in talking about anger thus far, we have the idea that it's automatic, that humans react with anger differently, and that anger always involves blame.

Sometimes the anger passes quickly. This is normal and more healthy. But sometimes the anger lingers. We might relive what made us angry over and over again. Yes, I will acknowledge at this point that most of our anger often comes from what someone else does or says. But it also comes from things happening that we think are unfair, as well as random events. But yes, when we think of anger, we often end up thinking of what a certain person said to us or did to us. We think about it non-stop for hours, days, weeks, months, maybe forever. This is a huge problem. It is a problem because this anger is making us miserable, and it's decreasing our productivity and focus.

Also, who is the anger harming? Is it harming the person who made us angry? No. Very often, the person who caused this does not even realize or think that we might be angry with them in this very moment. They are living their lives. However, we are not living our lives. We are stuck in anger. So the anger is hurting us. Why would we engage in anger if it's only hurting ourselves? Good question illogical humans.

Okay, so any number of things can make us angry. The anger is an automatic response. We usually have to blame something or someone. Additionally, the anger does not even hurt the person or thing we blame. The anger only hurts ourselves. The answer seems clear to me. We act more like aliens. We implement some logical thinking into our processing of anger.

When something happens to make you angry, expect and accept the automatic response of feeling angry. But then immediately remind yourself that the ONLY person who will suffer from the anger is

YOU. Then release that anger.

Easier said than done, you say? Perhaps. But we have coping mechanisms for things like that. If you need help releasing the anger, then engage a coping mechanism. Take a time out, go outside, do something else, listen to music, exercise. Whatever your effective coping mechanism is, engage it.

If you keep anger inside and never release it, it starts to pile up internally. When this happens, you will find that you become angry more often, and from smaller things. Eventually, some anger will be forced to release, and it is usually released in fits of rage. Rage is uncontrolled anger. Rage is when the anger builds up too much pressure, and the top explodes. Rage is always a bad idea. I have never had anyone tell me that something good happened from an attack of rage. In fact, it is the opposite. Rage can cause physical damage, mental damage, damage to your career, and damage to your relationships. At this point, you would be starting to destroy your life because of rage, which had resulted from anger you never released.

Please do not destroy your life by letting anger fester inside your mind constantly, such that you are not living and enjoying life. Please do not destroy your life by letting anger build into rage so that you do stupid things that ruin major components of your life such as career and relationships. Just don't.

Realize that anger is going to come, but that you NEED to release it. Use whatever coping mechanisms work for you. You might have to experiment a bit to find what works best. Do not give up in searching for an anger management procedure that works best for you. Let it go. You must let the anger go. It serves no productive purpose and will only ruin your life and leave you in pain. Let it go.

CHAPTER TWENTY
Worry, Anxiety, Panic

Many people find themselves in a near constant state of worry, anxiety, or panic. I am surprised at how little it is talked about in comparison to how frequently the problem afflicts people.

Maybe you are one of the people who have these constant thoughts rushing through your head, which you cannot seem to control. You are filled with thoughts of things that might go wrong, or thoughts of things that might go much worse than they are presently going. You might think about something horrible happening that is not at all likely to happen. Or you might think about something that is going somewhat poorly, but your mind starts to push it toward the worst-case scenario. You might feel uncomfortable and vulnerable at all times, even when logically you should feel safe and calm.

As if these thoughts are not unpleasant enough, they will eventually cause deeper and more exaggerated emotional issues. The end result can be that you are uncomfortable leaving your home, traveling, being around others, being in the dark, being alone, or doing certain activities. You might develop OCD type symptoms or disorders. You might become depressed or socially uncomfortable. Any way you slice it, you become miserable, and you are no longer able to live life to the fullest. The struggle is real. It's no joke and it is much more serious than most people realize. This can plunge people into a deep pain that does not easily go away.

First, let us take a look at what we are dealing with. The chapter title and the topic consist of three different words, and we need to distinguish between each of them. In my view, they each indicate a different level of the same problem, from least severe to most severe.

Worry is the more mild of the three. Everyone worries. Worry is the human mind's way of indicating concern for an important issue. Worry is also a way for the human mind to remember important items. Worry is a tool. Yes, worry is unpleasant, but similar to touching a hot stove, it gives us a strong enough stimulus so that we will notice and take something seriously. I view worry as necessary. However, everything in moderation, right? It is not healthy to worry all the time. It leaves the mind in a constant state of dismay. It would be like if the pain from touching a hot stove was constant and never went away. It would no longer be useful as a protection safety tool. So while worry is a necessary human emotion for us to be fully functional and productive, it also needs to be kept under control.

Anxiety is one level above worry. While worry is more fleeting and variable, anxiety is more constant and intense. While worry is more of a warning system of something we should give attention to, anxiety is more of a mental illness. Anxiety is not trying to warn us of anything. Anxiety is just trying to torture us and make us miserable. Anxiety is trying to paralyze us so we can't function normally or enjoy life. Anxiety steals our freedom and takes away our ability to experience joy and happiness. Anxiety needs to be dealt with and eradicated if possible.

Panic is the most severe and intense of the three. Panic is acute anxiety. Panic is anxiety that spikes into a very intense peak. Panic is more psychotic than worry and anxiety, because the person has very little control over it. Panic is usually very unpredictable and comes with little or no warning. Panic attacks are so unpleasant they can completely debilitate a person and place them in the worst possible state of mind. The pain from panic is quite real and very intense. If worry is brushing your hand quickly across a hot stove, and anxiety is touching the stove and leaving your hand there, panic is like one of your fingers being burned off. Panic is unexpected, fast, severe, and intensely painful. Additionally, the lasting effects from panic result in a traumatic emotional injury. Worry can go away. Anxiety can subside for a time. But panic gives us PTSD so that we keep experiencing the pain from it even when it's not present. Panic requires treatment or it can lead to accidents or suicidal tendencies.

You can decide which of the three you experience. We won't focus on worry because worry is a natural useful human tool. If you worry too much, you need to moderate that with the ideas we are about to explore. However, anxiety and panic need our full attention. If your anxiety and panic is out of control and you feel you cannot function properly during a normal day, or you are having thoughts of suicide, you should talk to your doctor and see if medication is a good option for you. Since I am not a doctor, I am going to leave that to them. Instead, I am going to focus on the mental strategies of dealing with anxiety and panic.

As with depression, anxiety and panic (we will lump them together for now) is a monster that lives inside your head. The goal of the monster is to make you miserable, control you, and destroy you. So its mission is clear and obvious. It will whisper things in your head to trigger you into anxiety and panic. It learns what buttons to push and knows what to whisper in order to trigger you into a reaction. If you have anxiety or panic disorder, you already know what I am talking about, and that there are certain thoughts that trigger you more than others. Whenever these thoughts are whispered into your mind by the monster, you react with major anxiety or panic.

The strategy for fighting this involves using the monster's greatest enemies. Let's think. The monster whispers certain irrational thoughts in your mind that you then react to. So let us do the opposite of the monster. First, try not to listen. When you hear those whispers and trigger words or thoughts, just think "no, not listening." The monster will try repeating them. You will have to keep repeating your "no" response. The monster depends on you listening to what it whispers. Therefore, do not listen.

Secondly, the monster usually uses irrational thoughts. It tries to get you to believe these horrible ridiculous unlikely things are going to happen. The monster depends on irrational thought to control you and get a reaction from you. So do the opposite. Use logic. Instead of immediately reacting to the irrational thoughts, step back for a moment and examine the thought objectively. Ask yourself what evidence exists to prove that this thought is even likely to happen. If there is no good evidence, and it is not likely to happen, then you have invalidated the monster's thought by using logic.

The whole point is for you to take control of your mind back from the monster. Do not let the monster use irrational thoughts to trigger you into an episode of anxiety or panic. You have to fight back. Do not listen to the monster. Dismiss the monster. Tell it to go away. Use logic to clearly realize that what the monster whispers is not that realistic or likely to happen. If it is not realistic or likely to happen, then why worry over it?

Finally, develop coping mechanisms that work for you. This is especially important when dealing with panic disorder. Think of a panic attack as an epileptic fit. It comes on suddenly and you must have a clear plan and routine for how you try to deal with it. Some examples of coping mechanisms for anxiety and panic attacks include getting out of bed and walking around, going outside for a walk, listening to music, turning on the TV to a show that captures your full attention, or calling a friend. Getting into your car for a drive or starting up your chainsaw is not something you want to do. So be mindful that you are in a fragile state when you are dealing with an episode, but you really need to take action immediately. Continuing to lie in bed or sit in your chair is not a good idea. Immediately move and put your coping mechanisms into motion.

As with most things, I realize all of this is easier said than done. You really need to be serious about it and come up with action plans that work for you. You also need to practice all of the skills and methods we discussed. You might not succeed the first few times. That is to be expected, and is part of the process. Each time you fail, immediately review and consider what exactly did not work right. Then make a small change to plug that hole in the action plan. Eventually the methods will start to work for you. You have to retrain your mind to not be under the control of the monster. It takes time. You can do it.

I know those afflicted with worry, anxiety, and panic suffer a great deal. I know you try to put up with it. You might even try to keep it a secret from those around you. But please know that I and others understand that you are in pain from this, and people are likely willing to help you if they understand what you are going through. These disorders are not something you must live with forever. Absolutely not! There is hope, and I am certain you can improve your situation if you take steps to deal with it. You can beat this!

CHAPTER TWENTY-ONE
The Hunter Equation

Those of you who have read the book, *The Hunter Equation,* or *Rising to Greatness,* know what the Hunter Equation critical thinking tool is. Feel free to skip through this chapter, but stick with us if you feel a refresher course would be helpful. For those of you not familiar with the Hunter Equation, I need to explain what the actual Hunter Equation is. I am no longer talking about the book by the same name. I am talking about the actual Universal life equation called the Hunter Equation.

The Hunter Equation is a life equation that came through to me from the wisdom of the Universe after years of frustration over The Law of Attraction. I was never a fan of The Law of Attraction because I recognized early on that The Law of Attraction was flawed and incomplete. The Law of Attraction indicates that your thoughts bring you your results. Meaning, if you think positive thoughts, you will receive positive life results. Millions of people embraced this theory because their positive thoughts made them feel better and seemed to bring them more positive results in their life.

I obviously have nothing against people feeling better and receiving better results in their life. But I felt most of the hype was just based on the positive results side, and ignored the negative results side. Basically, people would give Law of Attraction credit when they received good results, but never said anything if it did not work out. Also, I knew that having positive intents and taking positive actions, was not enough to yield positive results in your life consistently.

The Law of Attraction also warns that if you have negative thoughts or intents, negative things will come into your life. A few things bothered me about this. I felt it was a bit narcissistic and gaslighting because The Law of Attraction essentially blames you if bad things happen to you. The Law of Attraction indicates that you must have had a negative thought that brought you your negative result. I raise the example of children who get cancer. Did these innocent children have a negative thought that resulted in them getting cancer? Are the children to blame for their own cancer? Of course not! Law of Attraction proponents would say that children getting cancer has nothing to do with Law of Attraction. They might even say that most bad things that happen to you have nothing to do with Law of Attraction. My argument is that if this is the case, then are they claiming that The Law of Attraction only works for positive things and not negative things? Is the Universe only one way? Does only good exist and bad does not? Does only light exist and darkness does not? Do life equations only have one side to them? Do any equations (math or otherwise) have only one side to them? Do we get to pick and choose what we believe, and just disregard all other truths, simply because we do not like them? So if I think a happy thought and something good happens, it is Law of Attraction in motion? And if I think a bad thought and something bad happens, it is Law of Attraction in motion? But if horrible things happen to good people with good thoughts, do we just ignore that part and pretend it does not exist? Also, when horrible people with horrible thoughts have great fortune happen to them, do we pretend that does not exist as well? Are we that unsophisticated and shallow? Do some only wear rose-colored glasses and pretend that is true reality? Yep, they do. Good for them. I am not here to tear down others or destroy The Law of Attraction. I am here to explain how The Law of Attraction is incomplete and does not reflect reality. I believe I received the complete life equation from the Universe that some would say completes the Law of Attraction.

For our purposes here, let's say the Law of Attraction is

BASICALLY saying that your OUTCOME is equal to your THOUGHTS/INTENT plus your ACTIONS. I know people have different views of the Law of Attraction and some would want to wrestle me in the weeds and parse words over it. But the above statement is an accurate BASIC understanding of the Law of Attraction. Based on the above statement, the Law of Attraction is based on two elements. Your Outcome = Intent + Actions.

The Hunter Equation adds additional elements to the equation. The Hunter Equation states:

FUTURE OUTCOME = INTENT + ACTIONS + EXTERNAL FORCES + RANDOM LUCK

The Hunter Equation adds the additional elements of External Forces and Random Luck to the life equation. For clarity sake, I am going explain each of the elements so we are very clear on how this equation works.

FUTURE OUTCOME - Your FUTURE OUTCOME is obviously your results. It can also be your goal. So if you had a goal you were trying to reach or achieve, you would put the goal or desired outcome into the equation as the Future Outcome. The Future Outcome can also be the unintended result of what you received.

INTENT - The INTENT is your intention and attitude. If you understand the Law of Attraction, then you understand what the Intent is. Intent means the same here as it does with the Law of Attraction. Intent is what you are intending and your attitude toward your intention.

ACTIONS - The ACTIONS are exactly what you think they are. These are the steps or actions you are taking. Actions can be positive, negative, or neutral. Actions are simply what you are doing.

EXTERNAL FORCES - This is the first new element I introduced, and likely the most important. EXTERNAL FORCES are all the things that can happen outside of your control. We do not directly control External Forces. We do not live in a vacuum, and sometimes things surrounding us affect us. Sometimes it does not matter how positive your thoughts and attitudes are, bad things can still happen, or we get results we did not anticipate. An example of an External Force would be when we are doing a great job at work, the boss loves us, we have a great attitude, great thoughts, and everything is going great; but then the company gets bought out and you get fired because of the restructuring. That is an External Force. You have no control over it, and there is nothing you could have done to avoid it. Life happens. Conversely, your boss giving you an unexpected raise can also be an External Force because it was mostly out of your control and not anticipated, yet it will have a major impact on your situation.

Health issues outside our control are other External Forces. Things that happen to our family members that change our lives are External Forces. So much of life is a result of External Forces. It does not matter how great your thoughts and attitudes are. THIS is the reason I think Law of Attraction can be a bit narcissistic or gaslight you. Law of Attraction might say that you somehow could have avoided bad things happening to you if you had a more positive outlook, thoughts, intentions, or what have you. But we can clearly see there are plenty of instances where bad things happen completely outside our control, regardless of how positive our thoughts were. Basically, the Law of Attraction will blame you for your misfortune, saying it's your fault because of your thoughts, or even actions. Sometimes, things that happen to us are NOT our fault. Tell that to soldiers who get their leg blown off. Tell that to the kids who gets cancer. MANY things are NOT in our control or our fault. Our thoughts are irrelevant in many cases. External Forces take this Universal truth and reality into account. Any life theory that does not account for External Forces outside our control is simply not based in reality.

RANDOM LUCK - This is the second element I

added. RANDOM LUCK is controversial because some people do not believe anything is random. Some people believe there is a reason for everything, and everything is based upon your destiny and pre-ordained design. I disagree fully. I believe that there is a random element in the Universe. If you put a bunch of jellybeans in a jar, close your eyes, reach in, and pull one out, was that jellybean randomly chosen, or was it pre-ordained that it would be chosen? Yes, some of you will argue with me until the end of time that the one jellybean you chose was meant to be chosen from the beginning of its existence. We will have to agree to disagree. Do you also believe every time you throw dice, that the outcome is pre-ordained? Do you also believe the world is flat? From a scientific point of view, I believe there is a random component because the Universe is always expanding, black holes changing, things growing, things dying, things being born. All these organic changes ensure there are constant VARIATIONS and VARIABLES in the Universe. These variables allow a random component to exist. But back down here to our reality, it just makes sense that some things are random. To be honest, I explain all of this in much more detail and in-depth in *The Hunter Equation* book. But I am hoping I have adequately made my case so you will at least accept the possibility of a random component so that we can move forward with the equation. In summary, Random Luck is that element that not only do we not control it, but nobody controls it.

That is the Hunter Equation. So how can we use it to our benefit? We use the Hunter Equation to help us set goals, analyze outcomes, contingency plans, anticipate possible external forces, and to make choices in an orderly logical way. The Hunter Equation is a useful tool for problem solving and decision making in everyday life, so it's helpful for you to understand how to use it. Let's go through an example of how to apply the Hunter Equation.

Assume for a minute you want to start your own business. As you set this goal, create your plan, and prepare to take the leap, you might want to engage the Hunter Equation first. As a reminder, the Hunter Equation is:

FUTURE OUTCOME = INTENT + ACTIONS + EXTERNAL FORCES + RANDOM LUCK

So let's start filling in the equation. The FUTURE OUTCOME is your goal. So the Future Outcome will be "Your New Business." This will hopefully be the desired end-result of all your efforts.

The INTENT is going to be your very positive thoughts and intention for this new business. Your Intent might include the fact you are doing this new business to help other people and make their lives better and easier. Your Intent would include your desire to provide excellent customer service. The Intent would include your intention of loving what you do and enjoying your work. The Intent is all the love and passion you have. The Intent needs to be positive obviously.

The ACTIONS are all of the steps required to make this business happen. The Actions will basically be your business plan. The Actions will be your step-by-step plan and task list. An important note is that the Actions element itself is also subject to the entire Hunter Equation. What I mean by that is when we look at the Actions, you need to also have the correct positive Intent toward each of the Actions. You also need to keep in mind the Actions are subject to External Forces hitting them, as well as Random Luck.

The EXTERNAL FORCES in this case will be all the possible things that can go wrong or go right. The External Forces portion is where you sit down and ANTICIPATE any and all possible things that can happen. Examples might be like "what if the bank does not support me," "what if the similar business to mine across town decides to attack me," "what if my sales are slower than I expect," "what if business is so amazing that I can't keep up," etc.

The External Forces is your time to consider all possible weird things that can happen, and start planning what your contingency plans will be. CONTINGENCY PLANS are critical in anything you do in life. You must expect anything and plan for everything. Do not be scared, be ready. Examining the External Forces up front provides you an opportunity to give your plans more in-depth thought, and at least have some back-up plans formulated. Looking at External Forces will also flush out some flaws in your plan so that you can make adjustments before you encounter the problem.

Next, you will consider the RANDOM LUCK factor. Good luck and bad luck both exist. Things might go better than expected. Great. Things also might go worse than expected. Be prepared. The Random Luck factor keeps you grounded in reality. How many people have you seen had their head in the clouds about something, and then got wiped out because something went wrong? Considering the Random Luck factor in your equation keeps you realistic and aware that something totally weird and unexpected might happen, and that you need to be ready and willing to accept and deal with such an eventuality.

That is your equation filled out, but you are not done yet. Now you can use the equation to try and improve your situation and chances for success. For example, you will examine EACH OF YOUR ACTIONS, and see how much any of those Actions are vulnerable to External Forces or bad Luck. If you find Actions that are super vulnerable or have a high likelihood of having negative External Forces or bad luck, you might want to consider altering those Actions so they are less vulnerable. Additionally, you can look at the possible External Factors you listed and see if some of those External Forces can be AVOIDED UP FRONT by taking certain other Actions before you start. This is where looking ahead helps you anticipate certain things and improve your chances. You can also look at your Random Luck element. Is there some possible item of bad luck you are afraid might happen? If so, are there any Actions you can take to lessen the chances of bad luck, or increase the probability of good luck? Furthermore, are there any possible GOOD External Factors you can proactively engage with to help your situation? For example, maybe you know a friend who can provide a very good recommendation or referral for you. The friend doing that would be an External Force (since it is outside your control), and that External Force would be very positive for you.

I do not want to get you totally lost in a maze of weeds. I could go on for days doing this, twisting and turning, and going backwards and forwards with this equation. I am hoping you are seeing how that is done, and you can realize how to do it. Going up and down the equation, forwards and backwards, is a great way to flush out flaws in your plan, and to add things that will improve your plan.

The Hunter Equation is relevant to your healing process in this book because it can also be used for personal relationships and personal issues. For example, let us say you want to lose weight. The Future Outcome would be "lose 20 pounds." The Intent would be your positive intentions for becoming healthier, feeling better, living better, and just being happier and more positive. You would be excited and enthusiastic about your intention for this goal. The Actions will be your exact plan of action of how you will lose the weight, such as a certain diet and exercise program. The External Forces will be the possible problems to crop up such as going to a party where there is the best-looking cake ever. What is your contingency plan if you find yourself in such a difficult tempting situation? Make sure you take into account these External Forces and have a contingency plan or coping mechanism in place to deal with it up front. Also, realize that Random Luck could dish out some bad luck at any time. For example, maybe you sustain an injury that will halt your exercise program. What then? Realize this is possible and perhaps give greater caution to lessen the chances of you getting injured, but also accept it could happen, and have a contingency plan in place if it does happen.

Again, I could go on for days with examples, but I hope you can see how the Hunter Equation can be helpful in setting up action plans within your recovery from various traumas. It forces you to break down goals, problems, and solutions, in an organized logical way. It allows you to see potential problems ahead of time so you can make changes to your plans up front. Making better and clearer choices can help us recover and heal from traumas and setbacks more quickly. It is helpful in organizing your thoughts, anticipating issues, making contingency plans, and increasing your chances of success. This is why applying the Hunter Equation is a helpful tool in healing.

CHAPTER TWENTY-TWO

Structured Task-Driven Lifestyle

If the Hunter Equation is a critical thinking, goal setting, and decision-making tool, a "structured task-driven lifestyle" is an action lifestyle tool used as a coping mechanism to get through daily life. Those who work with me personally know I am always preaching this as the first go-to tool when it comes to pulling us out of a depression or a major setback that has us paralyzed and broken. I wanted to include this concept in the book because some of you might be able to use it in getting productivity back into your life after having suffered a major loss or trauma.

After life deals us a major blow and throws us to the ground, we are often down for the count. When we feel beaten down, defeated, depressed, and hopeless, we often do not have the strength to get back up again. This means we might lay around the house a lot, ignore our tasks and responsibilities, and become very unproductive. If left unchecked, this can lead to problems with work, school, relationships, finances, and home life. When we lose the desire and strength to function properly, we lose our lives as we know it. What was a personal tragedy or setback, can turn into something that ruins our lives.

You absolutely cannot let that happen. You must take action to save your present lifestyle and future life. I have found the best way to do this is to institute a *structured task-driven lifestyle*. When everything has fallen apart, you have given up, and you cannot function properly, the best thing to do is create a structure that can carry you through, as long as you follow a simple regime.

The structured task-driven lifestyle is based upon a very simple, balanced, daily, and weekly program that is easy to follow and prompts you to do the productive tasks that must get done, while also including self-care and treats for helping your recovery. The structure is different for everyone. But I will lay out a very common structure so that you get the idea. The premise is that you will set up a schedule and list of tasks a week in advance, and a day in advance.

Let us take a look at a daily schedule first. The ingredients for any given day should include the following:

1. Morning wake up time and ritual
2. Morning task(s)
3. Exercise
4. Time outside
5. Meals you enjoy
6. Afternoon task(s)
7. Daily treat
8. Personal time
9. Evening ritual and bedtime
10. Sleep

Morning wake up time and ritual: It is important to have a set time you wake up each morning. It is very critical this first step is done correctly because it sets the tone for the day. If you mess this up, you will likely lose some of the discipline instilled within this lifestyle coping tool. Once you wake up, you need to jump right into your morning rituals. That might include feeding the pets and having your morning coffee. Check your messages and get the house opened up and ready for the day. The point of this step is to start out disciplined, but in a very gentle way. Self-care is important, and two cups of coffee or five minutes to sit staring out the window is totally allowed. This step will also include getting dressed and ready for your day. I mention this step specifically, because changing out of your bed clothes tells your mind and body it's day time and time to get busy. After this step you are ready for prime-time, even if you don't feel ready.

Morning task(s): This is when you look at the task list you completed the night before and jump right into completing those tasks. I often call this the "heavy lifting" of the day. Whatever needs to be done that day that you don't want to do, needs to be done at this time. It is helpful to not give it any thought or hesitation before jumping into this. Just start in. Yeah, you won't feel like it, you won't want to do it, you will think of excuses not to do it, but this is likely one of the most critical step of the entire day. You must jump in and do these tasks assigned for the day. You will eventually learn that it feels good to do them, and it feels good to do them early, because your day gets easier after this step. This is likely the most unpleasant part of your day. But these things need to get done, and doing them will make you feel better.

Exercise: I realize this might not be everyone's favorite topic, and that some of you might not include exercise in your lifestyle at all. I am not including exercise in your day because I think you are out of shape or need to lose weight. Nope. I am including it because exercise is one of the best treatments for depression and many other mental challenges. Exercise is a key treatment in your recovery from whatever set you back. I don't care what kind of exercise you do. I am not here to judge you or set an agenda for your fitness. For some of you, exercise might mean walking around your yard for twenty minutes. For others it might mean running several miles. For others it might mean doing twenty sit-ups, and for others it might mean going to the gym. You can spend some time in a pool if you have one handy. You can sit on a stationary bike watching TV. You can do whatever floats your boat. But exercise gets you active so that the mental demons are kept at bay. Exercise kind of re-engages you back into an active life. So whether it be for only ten minutes or for three hours, please slide it into your daily schedule wherever it is most convenient or works best for you.

Time Outside: Time outside is another of the most effective treatments for depression and anything that ails you. There is something magical about the effects of fresh air and sunlight. If you are clever, you might combine your exercise with your outdoor time. The outdoor time is critical, and even if it means sitting on your front steps for five minutes, please do it. Again, I am not telling you how much or how intense to engage in all the steps. I am just saying to do all the steps in some fashion. If you do, you will soon realize the value of doing them.

Meals You Enjoy: Everyone needs to eat. Obviously, it is helpful if you eat healthy. With that said, there is one requirement to this step. It is that you eat something you enjoy. I find it is very helpful if your meals are something you look forward to. So even if you are on a diet or specific meal plan, be sure to include something you enjoy. Mealtime is something to look forward to and enjoy, almost as an incentive.

Afternoon task(s): I find it helpful to break up your daily task list by placing an item or two early in the day, and then another later in the day. The morning ones should be more difficult and unpleasant so that the tasks later in the day are easier. Of course, you may choose to do all your tasks at once earlier in the day. That's fine. But it is also fine to break it up so that your morning tasks don't seem too overwhelming.

Daily treat: A daily treat is very important. You always need something, or multiple things, to look forward to every day. A treat for yourself is also part of your self-care in recovery. It doesn't matter what it is. You might combine your daily treat with your meals. You might allow yourself a favorite beverage in the evening. You might get an ice cream treat after your exercise. It's up to you. But institute something that you enjoy and that you will look forward to every day.

Personal time: Personal time is free time to do what you want in a leisure way. This might be spending time online, watching your favorite TV shows, listening to music, reading, or just sitting quietly. It is important for you to have some "down time" every day. I find it most useful when the personal time is done at the end of the day when you are unwinding after your long day. This is your time to slow down and feel good about all you did that day.

Evening ritual and bedtime: This is the opposite of the morning ritual. The first thing you want to do is make sure you complete your task list for the next day. You will need it in the morning. Do not wait to do the task list in the morning. When you wake up, your routine needs to be automatic. Other than doing your task list for the next day, this is a time for shutting down. Do any evening self-care, final TV show, or whatever it is that prepares you for a good night's sleep.

Sleep: Proper sleep is very important. Without proper sleep, you won't be able to do anything on this list correctly, and you will be a mess. Your bedtime should be pretty well set in stone, and be sure to give yourself enough hours sleep to feel ready in the morning.

So there you have it. Those are the ingredients for a well-balanced productive day. Yeah, yeah, some of you are ready to criticize the routine I laid out because you have a regular day job or you have kids to take care of. I fully realize this. I was using this daily routine as an example to show how it works. You have to construct a schedule that works for your specific situation. Everyone's schedule will be a bit different. But it's important you include all of the items on the list.

That brings us to the next part of the discussion. How you order and implement all of the ingredients is what I call "the arc of the day." The arc of the day is an attempt to create a natural arc with all the ingredients so that your day flows smoothly, productively, with the least amount of misery, and the most amount of joy.

Imagine an arc, like a rainbow. At the bottom is the morning when you wake up. The arc starts at the ground. You are just starting out. Then you start to climb up the arc. This is when you are doing your heavy lifting of morning tasks for the day. Not easy. But then you get past that and reach the peak or top of the arc. This is where you might be doing your outside time, exercise, or lunch. You are well into your day and your heavy lifting climb up the arc is behind you. Now you will begin descending down the other side of the arc. This is when you might be doing an easier task, having some personal time, or enjoying dinner. Finally, the downside of the arc touches the ground again and you are going to bed.

The idea of "the arc of the day" is to make sure the arc is working well for you. Do not put something difficult and miserable on the downside of the arc. Don't try to do something difficult right when the arc is about to touch ground again for the night. Make sure you are doing something satisfying at the top of the arc. Now you see why I inserted the more difficult unpleasant tasks at the beginning of the day when you are climbing up the arc. All your ingredients should fit naturally into the daily arc if possible.

If you have a regular day job and cannot do this, then what you can do is create mini arcs. For example, you will have one mini arc in the morning, then your regular workday, then another mini arc after work. So if you get out of work toward the end of the day, you would be starting up the front side of the mini arc. So do your most difficult task right after work. Then perhaps your exercise or whatever at the peak of your arc, then make your way down the easier backside of the arc as you aim toward bedtime. The arc of the day idea still works. You just might have to have smaller arcs, or a couple different arcs each day.

Everything I described above is in creation of a daily arc. You also need to construct a weekly arc. The concept is exactly the same for the weekly arc as it was for the daily arc. We will say that Monday morning is the bottom of the front side of the arc, and Sunday night is the bottom of the backside of the weekly arc. So how would you build this arc? Well, Monday and Tuesday we are climbing up the front side of the arc. So Monday and Tuesday might be the days we put our least pleasant tasks. Wednesday and Thursday are the days where we are reaching the peak of the arc. Hopefully by then you have completed your worst tasks of the week. Perhaps Wednesday and Thursday are good days for going out and doing something social, or some weekly activity you enjoy. Then Friday, Saturday, and Sunday you are climbing down the backside of the arc. Ideally, you would put in your easiest most enjoyable tasks and activities here. Be sure later on Sunday you start to wind down the week so you can prepare for another week. Sunday would be the day to do a task list for the upcoming week. Hopefully you get the idea.

Again, if you have a work schedule or something that messes with this structure, you can still use the arc of the week idea by instituting multiple arcs. For example, if you do all your weekly tasks on the weekend, you would have a mini arc that just covers Saturday and Sunday. So use that as your arc. You might guess by now that I would suggest doing your most difficult tasks Saturday morning, and then being more leisurely Sunday afternoon.

Yes, people also do monthly arcs. Some people have a monthly task list and tackle everything difficult the first part of the month, and then do something special toward the end of the month. The possibilities are endless. If you find yourself wanting to do a yearly arc or ten year arc, then we might have to discuss a potential compulsive disorder haha. But I'm all for it if you can sell its benefits and make it help you in great ways.

I am truly hoping you see the benefit of using such a structured approach to help recovery from depression and traumas. If we do not have any approach at all, it is possible we end up motionless for weeks and months, or even years. People can lose everything if they do not pick themselves back up again. My structured "task driven lifestyle and arc of the day approach," is a way for people to construct something they can blindly follow that will put them onto a path to recovery much faster. In addition, you will be functioning properly and taking care of your responsibilities so that you do not make your situation worse than it already is. With this tool, you will be back up and running, and perhaps end up more productive than you ever were before. I hope it can help you in some way.

CHAPTER TWENTY-THREE
Fear

Although we cannot tackle all the possible sources of trauma in one book, we absolutely must discuss the one element that is present in all traumas and sources of pain. Fear. Fear is a common enemy, even among those who are not suffering from trauma. Fear puts everyone in pain in some way. Therefore, developing the ability to manage fear is a life tool everyone should acquire.

Fear is one of the most basic human emotions. In the earlier days of humanity, fear was a very necessary emotional response tool. Fear was a warning sign to take precautions. Obviously, humans were vulnerable to many dangers including predators, other humans, weather, lack of basic needs such as food and water, and pretty much any environmental factor that could jeopardize safety. Fear made humans stay in shelter when it might be unsafe to go out. Fear made humans take flight from predators or other humans that would harm them. Fear made us stay vigilant in collecting food and resources. Without fear humanity would not have survived. I am almost making it sound as if fear has been a hero of humanity.

However, as civilization evolved, many human vulnerabilities faded away. For the most part, humans did not have to be totally consumed by the prospect of being randomly eaten by a lion on any given night. Humans developed systems for making sure food and water were always available. Humans had much more sophisticated shelters to protect them from the weather and other hazards. Fear became a bit less necessary. Of course, being attacked by other humans was still a cause for fear. Fear also helped humans avoid obvious bad choices.

As the need for fear as a basic protection subsided, humans also became more intellectually advanced. Humans recognized the power fear had over others. If you could say the right thing, you could scare others into doing things you wanted them to do. Fear started being used as a weapon. Ever since then, fear has been weaponized in ever changing ways, and this has remained the same throughout time. The saying, "The more things change, the more they stay the same" applies to the concept of fear. Humanity through the modern ages has always found ways to manipulate human thinking while using fear as the basic tool for doing so.

While most humans no longer fear being eaten by a lion while they sleep at night, they do fear losing things they have, or losing their lifestyle, culture, traditions, advantages, routines, and basically anything they have become accustomed to. That makes fear very easy to use against someone. I can simply look at your life, everything you have, and everything you do, and I can present you with a scenario that you might lose one of those items. You will then fear that idea. Once you fear that idea, I can present you with a solution to avoid it and you will buy into it. Or I can manipulate you to do something or give something in order to avoid it. Whether I use the "carrot or the stick," I can use fear to make you do what I want.

This weaponization of fear has caused trauma to people over time. People now fear fear. People know that fear equals loss. Fear equals pain. But at the same time people keep responding to fear as a weapon being used against them. It is a cycle of abuse that snares a person into being trapped by fear. You fear having fear used against you, while you fear losing what fear is threatening to take from you. You fear doing anything that might cause you to have fear used against you, or fear losing something, or you maybe fear being in fear even though you are already in fear thinking about fear.

So we just went from fear being a useful necessary tool of early humanity, to fear being weaponized and used against us with or without factual justification. After a point, we do not even fear what fear might bring. Rather, we just fear fear and feel afraid whenever fear might come knocking. We fear everything for every reason, and no reason. We become mentally ill with fear. We are consumed with fear.

Almost every person today is consumed by fear to some degree. Perhaps it is on a sliding scale. Plenty of people live their lives in minimal fear, but even more live their lives in great fear. Or what I should say is that plenty of people do not live their lives because of fear. Fear has become irrational. We stop doing things because of fear, even if we don't fully reason through or comprehend what we are afraid of exactly. We just avoid things that give off a hint of fear.

We fear the unknown. We don't know why. We just fear it. So anything not completely defined consumes us with fear. This can cause us to not do things or not experience things just because we are not totally certain what will happen. Well, since nothing in our future is certain, that means everything is uncertain and unknown. This means some people reason out that they should do absolutely nothing in order to avoid the unknown, and thus avoid fear. That is on the extreme end of the scale.

Others do not fear everything unknown but fear certain things. People fear many of the topics in this book. People fear failure, broken relationships, someone they love dying, being hurt or abused, making mistakes, being lonely, getting sick, and the list goes on. Now you see why fear plays a part in every subject within this book. The reason we need to discuss fear, is because as long as we are controlled by fear, we cannot fully recover from our traumas.

When you work toward recovering from trauma in your life, you must first release any fear you have toward that trauma. For example, if you were sexually assaulted, an integral part of your recovery is to release the fear that you will be assaulted again at any moment by the next person who walks past you. You cannot possibly recover from that trauma while living in that fear.

You cannot recover from a major failure in your life if you are consumed by the fear that you will just keep failing. If you hold onto that fear of failure, you will just be afraid that everything you do will fail. If you think this way, you won't try again, try other things, or try at all. You will have given up trying because of your fear of failure. This makes it impossible to recover from your traumatic life event involving a failure or setback of some sort.

Of course, I could go on and on and list every possible trauma and scenario of why recovery from trauma is impossible without releasing the fear of it first. But there is one more example I want to discuss. The fear of death. This is important to discuss because the fear of death is a core issue of fear that most humans have. It is the one holdout that most humans can't shake off from their psyche. You might be able to shake off your fear of failure, of being attacked, or finding a dead mouse in your chicken nuggets, but many people have trouble shaking off their fear of death. For this reason, the fear of death is still a vulnerability that not only can be used against you, but can also be used by yourself against yourself.

Even if we pretend that the entire world will leave you alone and cause you no harm, there is still this fear of death that your mind may use to paralyze you from doing things. You might be unwilling to travel or fly in an airplane because of your fear of death. You might be afraid to leave your home because you fear getting sick, which then might result in death. You might be afraid of going outside because you are afraid of getting hit by a car or falling off a cliff. The possibilities are endless, and your fear of death can cause you to stop living. You will already be dead before you are dead. Your greatest fear might have been death, but you would already be living your greatest fear since your fear of death would have already caused you to stop living. This means you are as good as dead already. You might recognize this ridiculous paragraph is similar to the one further back about fearing fear. It is because this is what fear does. It gets us caught up in a mental knot so we cannot move.

One other point before we move on. Not only does fear prevent us from doing things and living life, but fear also opens us up to manipulation and abuse. Fear is a tool toxic people use to control us. Once a toxic person knows what we fear, they will use it to get control over our emotions through our door of fear. They will then manipulate us into doing whatever they want by holding our fears over our head against us. You will then be a slave and prisoner to the toxic abuser because you are a slave and prisoner to your fears.

Does anyone really want to live this way? What a nightmare. It is important you see how horrible all of this is. Why is that do you ask? It's because one of the most useful methods in eliminating fear, is showing yourself and reminding yourself that what fear does to you is far worse than the actual fear itself. For example, the fear of failure prevents you from trying anything. It means you stop progressing in your life. You will never advance in your life again. You are stuck. You are done. That's pretty horrible. I submit to you that trying something and failing is actually not as horrible a fate as being stuck and done forever because you tried nothing. You come to realize that the fear is worse than the possible outcome you are trying to avoid.

The ultimate extreme of this concept is to apply it to the fear of death. We have already established above that the fear of death can essentially cause you to stop living, such that you are basically already dead. Therefore, I suggest to you that doing things in life where there is a slight risk of death is actually not nearly as bad as doing absolutely nothing and already being dead since you are no longer living your life. This idea should give you pause, and prompt you to set your fear of death aside, and still take risks so that you are actually LIVING your life instead of doing nothing out of fear.

Okay, so the first concept is to realize that fear itself is actually worse than what you fear. There is no worse fear than fear itself. The second concept you should consider is facing your fears with facts. You should take whatever fear you have and drill down on what exactly about it you fear. For example, let's say you had a bad breakup. This results in you fearing relationships. You already know from our first concept that your fear of relationships could cause you to be alone for the rest of your life, which you might fear more than the possibility of another breakup. But maybe you need more convincing in order to deal with your fear of relationships.

Thus, consider what exactly it is about relationships you fear the most. Is it being lied to? Is it being cheated on? Is it having a broken heart again? Is it being alone again? Really think about it and drill down on the exact thing you are truly most afraid of regarding this issue of relationships. Let's say it turns out that you are most afraid of trusting and being cheated on. Okay, fair enough. So what you do is face that fear. Realize and accept that there is a chance you will be cheated on. It's accepting reality more than anything else. It Doesn't mean you will be cheated on, but means you could be. That's step one. The next step is to become more comfortable with the consequences of that. So come up with a plan of what you will do if you are cheated on. You might determine you will end the relationship, cry with some ice cream, change your furniture around, and then go for walks. Then perhaps you would start looking again. By thinking all of this through in advance, you have shown your mind that even if the worst happens to you, there is a clear plan you will follow, and YOU WILL BE OKAY. Once your mind sees that you will be okay, the fear subsides a bit.

Therefore, when facing your fears, first accept it can and might happen due to facts of reality. Then you want to reason it completely through so you are more comfortable with the worst-case scenario. In most cases, the worst-case scenario is still not as bad as letting the fear stop you from living your life.

Some of you might be thinking about the fear of death again. How can this possibly apply to the fear of death? How can you accept that death might or will happen? How can you reason through that the worst-case scenario of death happening is actually not as bad as the fear of death itself?

My answer is fairly simple. Death is going to happen. Right? So you have to accept what will happen. You have to learn to accept realities of all kinds. Also, you can reason through the worst-case scenario of death happening by using your spiritual or religious beliefs. If your spiritual or religious beliefs are of no comfort to you, that means you don't actually believe in your spiritual or religious beliefs. So you might want to take a look at that. We are not going to discuss spirituality or religion in this book. But it's something you need to explore. It is important for you to have a mindset where you are comfortable with your life and comfortable with your death. If you are not comfortable with either or both of these, then it is time to make some changes in your life. Maybe this book can help with that in some small way.

One thing for certain is that there is no issue more difficult or more evil than fear. What started out as a blessing at the beginning of humanity has turned into humanity's biggest vulnerability. When fear is around, you can be rest assured that evil is lurking not far behind. You are not seeking this. You are seeking love. Love is the total lack of fear. Love is unconditional. The term "unconditional" by default cannot include fear, since fear is by definition a *condition* under which we live when we don't have the trust or confidence to be unconditional in how we are living. If you eliminate fear, you have a better chance of finding love, feeling love, and living in love.

CHAPTER TWENTY-FOUR
Love & Empathy

Love is not a choice, or a tool, or a thing we decide to give or withhold. Love is a state of mind and state of being. Love is an energy. Love IS energy. Love is the energy of the universe that flows in perfect harmony and frequency. Love is when everything is the way it should be.

Imagine that perfect day where you sit on the edge of a field and some woods that overlook the water. You close your eyes. The temperature is perfect such that you cannot actually feel the temperature. It is in perfect synchronicity with your body so there is no sense of too warm or too cold. You hear the sounds of the field and the sounds of the woods at the same time. You hear the breeze, the birds, and the silence, all at the same time. You feel the breeze such that it makes it easier to breathe, but not so that it gives a chill or puts your hair out of place. Even with your eyes closed, it is as if you can still see the sun shining on your face, the light movement and swaying of the field grass, and the beautiful perfect ripples of the water below. You are present in your human form with your human malfunctions and human problems, yet in this moment you are only taking in the senses I am describing. You are one with nature. Your mind does not wander to any thoughts other than the perfection of all the senses in that moment. Everything is separate, yet everything is one, with each other, at the same time, including you, your senses, and your mind. All of this together is resonating at the same frequency in exact synchronicity, which creates a perfection of beauty that is beyond normal belief. No matter what else is going on elsewhere, everything is okay in this moment. This is life at its most perfect beautiful moment. This is love.

Now take that scene, picture, and scenario described above, and introduce another person into it. Introduce multiple people into it. The other people are like the field grass moving randomly with the breeze. There is no controlling the breeze. There is no controlling exactly how the field grass blows or moves. There is no controlling when the birds sound off and when they don't. These other people in this perfect environment cannot be controlled, but they are part of the environment, and are to be appreciated the same way as everything else in the environment.

Love is allowing those people to BE part of that environment in whatever way they choose to BE. A state of being is a state of existence in the moment. You do not control the state of being of other things. You just unconditionally accept how they are, and what they are. You do not become angry at the field grass for blowing in a certain degree angle of a direction. You just accept unconditionally its current state of being. This is love.

Love is an unconditional acceptance of a state of being. Sometimes a state of being might not be matched to your personal human preferences. You are allowed to have preferences. You are human after all. But love is when you unconditionally accept and appreciate someone's state of being, even if it is not matched to your human preferences.

You might like chocolate ice cream and I prefer vanilla ice cream. But I still love that you like ice cream. I love that you enjoy ice cream. I love that you love ice cream. You do not have to enjoy the same kind of ice cream I do in order for me to love you.

I might have certain human preferences of what physical features of other humans I find attractive. You don't have to have any of those features in order for me to love you. I do not need to be attracted sexually or otherwise in order to love you. I love you for your uniqueness of being. I might not like a certain length of field grass, but I still love and appreciate its existence, as it is part of the perfect fabric of beauty we experienced in the vision.

If you are field grass, I want you to be free to be you. If you are human, I want the same thing for you, but I also want you to be happy. I also want you to experience all the wonderful amazing diverse emotions humans can experience. You might be nothing like me, and we might not share any common human preferences, but I love you because I desire for you to be part of the perfect harmony of existence where you have the freedom to be who you are, and you are able to experience happiness and all other amazing human emotions.

My unconditional love means I do not put conditions upon my love for you, requiring you to meet certain preferences and traits. I just want you to be free to connect to the perfect harmony and frequency that surrounds us. We can all be totally different from each other and still be connected to the one and same environmental frequency.

So this is how we love people. We appreciate them and want the best for them, as they are enjoying the connection of beauty in whatever way they choose. There are no requirements to meet certain preferences. There is only one common desire to be in sync with the perfect beautiful frequency surrounding us all.

I can still love you even if I do not agree with your thoughts or ideas. I can still love you even if I have no desire to engage romantically with you. I can still love you even if your methods of doing things are completely different from mine. Even despite all the differences and contrasting preferences, I can still love you because I want the best for you. I want you to be part of the beauty and harmony in your own unique way.

This concept does not only apply to loving others. This concept applies to loving yourself. You may have experienced some of the traumas discussed in this book, or you may have experienced other traumas. These traumas may have affected the view you have of yourself. Perhaps in a perfect world you would have a preference of being perfect and making no mistakes in life. But perhaps now, you realize you have indeed made mistakes. So now, your preferences of being perfect are no longer met. Thus, perhaps you may have stopped loving yourself.

Please reconsider your judgments of yourself, and consider that you are worthy of love, the same as others are. As with loving other people, just because you don't meet your exact preferences does not mean you are not worthy of love. You too, deserve the freedom to be part of the perfect harmony and beauty of life, even if you do not meet all of your own preferences. Just because someone else or yourself is not perfect does not mean you should not be appreciated and loved enough to be connected to the frequency of all things around you, such that you can experience happiness, acceptance, and harmony.

Even if we are able to somehow accept the differences of others and love them, too often we are unwilling or unable to accept our own differences within ourselves, so that we can love ourselves. If we feel less than perfect, or if we feel we let ourselves or someone else down, we feel unworthy of unconditional love. This is wrong. This is not fair. This goes against nature and the universe. We love the field grass regardless of how the wind blows it. Even if you have acted, behaved, or turned out differently than you expected or wanted, you are still worthy of this universal unconditional love.

If you do not love yourself because you feel others do not love you, then you are missing the point of love again. Remember, love is not a choice, or something given or withheld by others. Love is a state of being. Nobody else gets to decide if you are worthy of love or not. The fact you exist in nature is proof and validation that you are worthy of love. As long as you desire to be part of the connection of oneness and the harmonic frequency of nature surrounding you, that gives you the right to love, and to be loved. If you are connected to, and within this state of being, then you are loved if you will allow it within you.

I ask you to consider how you see love. Look at how you decide when to love, or when not to love. Look at whether you love yourself. Examine if you are being judgmental and using too many preferences when deciding if to love or not. Evolve, grow, and realize that love is not to be seen this way. Love is a state of being, to be connected with, and become a part of. Love is energy. Be connected to this energy, feel this energy, and be part of this energy. Then you not only love, but you are love.

Empathy is having enough love and compassion for others that you are willing to feel what they feel. Sympathy is feeling bad for someone else out of an act of politeness. Empathy is going a step further and feeling what they feel, as if you were them.

If you lose a loved one, I can feel sympathy for you and know you are sad. I can feel bad that you have lost someone you love. But to feel empathy for you, I have to feel your thoughts and your pain. I have to feel that you actually feel lonely right now. I have to feel that your pain is deep and maybe you are not sure how you can keep going. I have to truly feel your loss so that I can understand your loss.

If I feel sympathy for you, I might buy a sympathy card and give it to you. But if I feel empathy toward you, I might not buy a sympathy card for you. Instead, I will sit next to you, listen to you, and comfort you. I will do this because my empathy showed me that you are feeling lonely, and that you do not know if you can survive the pain. My empathy knows to take away your loneliness and show you there is hope.

You can see how much more powerful empathy is. So imagine if we treat people around us with more empathy. Instead of judging something you said, I instead try and FEEL what you are feeling so that I know why you said the thing you said. What you said is not nearly as important as why you said it. Only with empathy can I explore why you said it. What emotions of fear or pain caused you to say what you said? Instead of replying to what you said, I can respond to why you said it, and relate to how you are currently feeling. This is a way more effective method of communication and human interaction.

For example, we might need to choose a color to paint a room. I choose white and you choose purple. You think white is boring and I think purple is ugly. At this point, we can choose to disagree, and we can argue, fight, or even stop speaking to each other. But instead, maybe I will use empathy and will try to understand how you FEEL about purple. I might ask you how purple makes you feel. You might then tell me that purple was your mother's favorite color, and ever since she died you have felt lost and in great pain. Painting the room purple would make you feel your mother is right there with you, and make you feel happier and give you comfort. After I truly understand how you FEEL, I can have empathy for you and realize that maybe purple is not ugly anymore. In fact, now that I have engaged my empathy for you and understand how you feel, maybe I see purple is kind of beautiful in a way. Perhaps we can do a light purple and then paint the trim white.

We should treat ourselves with the same empathy that we treat others. Maybe I am feeling lazy and I am angry with myself for being so lazy. But perhaps if I show myself some empathy and ask myself why I FEEL lazy, I will realize that I am lazy because I am sad. Maybe instead of being angry with myself for being lazy, I should show empathy toward myself, be compassionate toward myself, and engage in some self-care activities that will make me feel less sad. Then maybe after I feel better, I can be more productive.

We must treat ourselves with love and empathy as we would ideally treat others. I left this topic for last because treating yourself with love and empathy is the one treatment and cure that applies to all traumas in life.

I certainly hope you found our discussions and some of my suggestions and solutions helpful. But even if they have still left you feeling inadequate, you can always contemplate love and empathy for yourself. Also, the secret, which is not so secret, is that if you show love and empathy toward others, it will come back to you like a mirror image. Engaging with others in a state of love and empathy opens your mind and energies to receiving it also. It allows this love and empathy to flow within yourself. If I open a door to let energy out, this also allows energy from outside to flow in. So being loving toward others, allows others to be loving toward you. As we discussed above, it is not even about seeking or needing love from others. Being in the state of love allows you to be connected to that perfect harmony of love that surrounds us.

Things might sometimes seem ugly in that room where you are sitting, or ugly from those people surrounding you, but you can connect to the greater expanse that surrounds you. You can connect to nature far away outdoors. You can connect to people far from you. You can connect to the universe. You can connect to the souls of those no longer on Earth. You can be love, and you can connect with love. You can show empathy, feel empathy, and this very act of engaging with empathy is an act of love.

We covered many topics in this book. I hope you found some of them helpful and relevant to your own life, or the lives with whom you are connected. If you enjoyed this experience and process of healing, you might also consider my book, *Rising To Greatness*. In *Rising To Greatness* I go more in-depth within a step by step transformational process for those seeking to rebuild their lives and acquire more advanced life skills.

My desire and love for you is that you take your journey to become whatever you wish to become. I want you to feel connected to love from inside and outside. I want you to be protected from negative forces that would attempt to steal from you of your freedom or happiness. I wish to see you self-empowered so you have total freedom of expression and thought.

Let nobody take away your empowerment and freedom of thought.

Who is better than you? Nobody
Who has the right to hurt you? Nobody
Who has the right to be abusive toward you? Nobody
Who has the right to strip you of your dignity? Nobody
Who has the right to take away your self-respect? Nobody
Who has the right to define you as something you are not? Nobody

Despite your traumas, setbacks, wounds, and life experiences, you are a unique valuable individual. You are entitled to as many chances at life as you are willing to stand up for. You are entitled to freedom and choice. You are entitled to be loving and be loved. Please let your soul rise to new heights, and may your happiness and success result from your healing.

Also, by Brian Hunter

Rising To Greatness is the companion book to Heal Me, and is a self-help book that takes you on a step-by-step transformation, from the ashes of being broken and lost, to the greatness of self-empowerment, accomplishment, and happiness. This book includes such topics as developing your sense of self, eliminating fear from your life, mastering your emotions, self-discipline and motivation, communication skills, and so much more.

Surviving Life: Contemplations Of The Soul is a unique and powerful book full of compassion and empathy, which combines the issues of what hurts us the most, with thoughts and advice meant to empower us toward happiness and independence. *Surviving Life* is medicine for the soul. It guides us through our deepest pains and weaknesses, and leads us to a place of self-empowerment, inspiration, strength, and hope. The topics covered are raw, diverse, and very practical. *Surviving Life* includes many subjects, and answers many questions, such as, "What is your purpose on this planet?" "When you think nobody loves you," "How can you feel good?" as well as practical advice on battling depression, suicide, and figuring out who you truly are. *Surviving Life* is a practical and contemplative manual for people of all ages, and the perfect book for gifting to those who need guidance and love.

EVOLVE is a cutting-edge, unique, powerful, and practical personal transformation self-help improvement book, which examines human life and all of its issues from a unique futuristic approach with a touch of humor. A selection of topics include healing from personal losses and traumas, coping with sadness and depression, moving past the fear that others use to control, manipulate, and abuse you, finding clarity in thinking, advanced communication skills, evolving your relationships, exploring the meaning of life, how everything in the Universe is connected, developing your psychic ability, and a little discussion about aliens possibly living among us. Yes, there is everything, which is all directly tied back to your own personal life.

Living A Meaningful Life is an epic book series, with numerous installments, that will change your life. We are all capable of doing extraordinary things. We must only decide within ourselves to BE extraordinary. The Living A Meaning Life book series is a powerful story, and journey, of one such 'family' who dared to be extraordinary. By looking past their own obstacles in life, and choosing to always 'do the right things,' they became extraordinary within themselves, and this resulted in them doing extraordinary things that changed the lives of everyone around them, and their community. The main characters must navigate life struggles, both personal, and community oriented. They do so by 'doing the right things,' through exhibiting integrity, decency, generosity, and compassion. Life is never easy, people make mistakes, but there is nothing that can't be overcome when we have the courage to do what we know is correct and true within our soul.

The Hunter Equation is a practical spirituality book covering many topics, including life after death, reincarnation theory, cycle of life and death, human and animal souls, destiny vs. free will, synchronicities, Karma, soulmates, twin flames, angels, alien life, the future of humans, and many more topics. This is also the original book to unveil and fully explain the Hunter Equation life tool, and why it is far more relevant and accurate than The Law of Attraction.

The Walk-In is Brian's dramatic memoir that takes you on a personal life-long journey, from childhood, through coming-of-age discoveries, successes, failures, and deep depressions and struggles. The book describes paranormal events, resulting in the development of psychic abilities. This book is a very raw and honest adventure, which is not for the faint of heart, as it includes illicit scenes and themes.

ACKNOWLEDGMENTS

Thank you Sarah Delamere Hurding for your editorial assistance, encouragement, and endless support. Thank you to all of my clients and benefactors who have supported my mission of helping people become greater, stronger, more self-empowered, and free of pain.

Printed in Great Britain
by Amazon